FASCINATING WEXFORD HISTORY

Fascinating Wexford History

VOLUME ONE

A worthy follow-up to *Famous Wexford People in History*

by the same author, this is a book of surprises.

Chances are you'll find at least one surprising

fact on every page.

DES KIELY

PARSIFAL PRESS

Published by the Parsifal Press, Newry
Copyright © 2019 by Des Kiely

A CIP record for this title is available from The British Library

ISBN: 978-0-9933960-7-6

Special thanks to Eileen Cloney, Peggy Cowman,
Mick Cuddihy, Cathy Ffrench, Lorraine Galvin, Bill Kelly,
David M. Kiely, George Lawlor and Ian Magahy

Cover art and design by the author
Set in 10.5 Iowan Old Style by the author

To Mel, Michelle, Kathy, Simon and Lucy

ABOUT THE AUTHOR

Des Kiely is by profession a graphic designer living in Wexford. He can trace his family history back to the village of Stradbally in County Waterford and to the house where his great-great-great grandfather John Kiely was born in 1778. The family moved north to Derry and again back south to Dublin, then Wicklow, so Des has almost completed the journey back home to Waterford. His hobbies include photography, music, art and writing local history. This is his second book on Wexford history, the first being his bestselling *Famous Wexford People in History*.

CONTENTS

FOREWORD

It was the Antrim poet James Orr, The Bard of Ballycarry, who wrote the line "The savage loves his native shore." The line is indeed true in almost every instance and in Ireland can be evidenced in our ofttimes tribal passion for our place of birth. It is important to state that if we have no concept of our past or the manner with which people dealt with issues of yesteryear, then it is almost impossible for us to have an understanding of who and where we are, or indeed, where we are going.

By pure coincidence I pen these words on the same day that Irish Education Minister Joe McHugh has indicated that History is to be given a special status in our Junior Certificate cycle. This despite the advice of others deemed more incisive in the knowledge of the curriculum. History in Ireland has often created a divisiveness that has led to much rewriting or sanitizing of the facts. Indeed, even our current two main political parties are still regarded as having 'Civil War' differences despite being able to coalesce relatively tranquilly.

It can also be said however that when it comes to an understanding and indeed knowledge of our place many of us are bereft of actual and factual memoirs. The savage may indeed love his native shore but by the same token have little regard or knowledge of his or her place. It is therefore important that we salute Des Kiely and his literary persuasion, who present us with a myriad of historical insights into so much of our actual history.

This publication gives us stories of war, injustice, natural history, tragedy, compassion and heroism, all emanating from and occurring on the soil and shores around us or carried out principally by sons and daughters of Wexford. It depicts acts worthy of celebration or mourning. It questions official memoirs whilst casting an inquiring eye backwards.

Many of us, myself included, often bemoan the fact that we never put to paper or record in any way recounts or recollections of elderly relatives or neighbours or people of renown in our communities. Indeed, page 129 of this book features a story about a murder in Cinema Lane in Wexford where my own grandfather Eddie Hall was playing cards a mere plaster wall away from the crime. I never once spoke to my late grandfather about this incident, or sought his recollection of it, despite having knowledge of it happening from the time I was a child!

Des does us a great service in this regard with the publication of this book. His collection of 33 insights and retelling of happenings makes for delightful and often thought-provoking reading. The book's title *Fascinating Wexford History* doesn't leave us disappointed. The stories and recounts are all absolutely fascinating in every sense. For instance, the death of 14 souls at the Newtownbarry massacre during the Tithe War is one such piece of history that gives a clear insight as to how passion for the land and how injustice visited upon others builds comradeship amongst neighbours, but also clearly illustrates the sectarianism that blighted this entire island up to very recent times.

History constructs the foundations for strong and vibrant communities. No place really becomes a community until it is encased in memories, be they family stories or traditions or indeed civic events of remembrance. It can be said that without an awareness of its history a place hasn't really been formed.

From Baginbun to Bunclody and from Gorey to The Hook, County Wexford has history spanning many centuries coursing through the veins of its people. History that has aged through careful handing down through the generations. Often unpleasant, often transposed inaccurately to suit the listener. Whatever the interpretation it is imperative that we continue to immortalize these fascinating memoirs through printed matter for our children and their children to digest. This allows us to evolve as a people in the knowledge that our forebears, their acts and deeds, continue to form us as a community.

In presenting this record of various events of our past Des Kiely informs us of so much that has lain dormant or indeed unknown to many. A presentation of local historical events such as this is a most welcome addition to our reservoir of available references. It certainly helps to keep 'the heather blazin'.

George Lawlor
Mayor of Wexford

When Hitler's Luftwaffe bombed County Wexford

The aftermath of the bombing of the Shelburne Co-operative Creamery in Campile that killed three young women in August 1940, the first bombing of neutral Ireland by German aircraft during WWII. (photo: Military Archives)

WHEN the United Kingdom and her Allies declared war on Germany in 1939, the Irish Free State (officially renamed Éire or Ireland in the Constitution of 1937) remained neutral in what was called the 'Emergency'.

Between 1939 and 1942 a total of 83 manned Look Out Posts (LOPs) were constructed by the Irish Defence Forces along the Irish coast, from Louth to Donegal, to monitor any hostile activity. 'EIRE' markings were later added to warn both Allied and Axis aircraft that they were flying over neutral territory. The Wexford coast had seven LOPs and painted markings numbered 'EIRE 10' to 'EIRE 16'. These were located at Kilmichael, Cahore, Ballyconnigar, Greenore, Carnsore, Kilmore Quay and Hook Head.

Despite the efforts of the Coast Watching Service volunteers, German bombs were dropped on a number of locations close to the east coast of Ireland in 1940 and 1941. These included counties Louth, Meath, Dublin, Kildare, Carlow, Wicklow and Wexford.

CAMPILE, 26 August 1940:

At 1.40pm, two German Heinkel He 111 planes were observed approaching the Wexford coast through clear skies by the Greenore and Carnsore LOPs and continuing west, following the Rosslare-Waterford railway line.

One aircraft dropped four bombs over Ambrosetown, near Duncormick, missing the railway viaduct but damaging the cottage of Jem and Johanna Hawkins. Jem had been whitewashing his home when the bombs fell, two on either side of the house. The blasts swept the whitewash brush from his hand and was never seen again. All three people in the cottage escaped injury.

The second plane was seen approaching from the Ramsgrange direction before circling over Campile. It dived to an altitude of a couple of hundred feet before dropping four bombs. The Shelburne Co-operative Creamery canteen, situated close to the railway line, was hit and a railway siding was damaged, as was the house of the railway stationmaster Paul McCrohan, whose hens were killed. One of the bombs fell in a field close to a hotel owned by Mrs Johanna Hart, blowing out the windows.

It was an hour after the bombing and only following a roll call when it was discovered that three young women were under the debris of the Co-op canteen. The bodies of sisters Mary Ellen Kent and Kitty Kent from Terrerath near New Ross and Kathleen Hurley from Garryduff were found, identified

Members of the Defence Forces and rescue workers in the bombed-out Shelburne Co-op. (photo: Irish Press)

The victims of the Campile bombing, left to right: Mary Ellen Kent (aged 30), her sister Kitty (aged 26) and Kathleen Hurley (aged 27).

only by their clothing. They were the first casualties on Irish soil of a German warplane during the Emergency.

Claimed by the Germans to have been a navigational error, mistaking the Irish east coast for the west coast of Britain, Hitler's government paid £9,000 in compensation three years later following protests by the Irish authorities.

The official report on the bombings in the Military Archive shows that the authorities believed the Rosslare-Waterford railway and the Shelburne Co-op were deliberate targets. The Germans were aware of the Co-op's business transactions with German firms that ceased at the outbreak of the war. Poultry, rabbits and butter were also exported to England, sent by train to Rosslare and then shipped to Fishguard. Ships between Rosslare and Fishguard had already been attacked off Tuskar Rock by German planes, indicating the

The Shelburne Co-operative Creamery had been built in 1919.

This is the site where the bombed Shelburne Co-operative Creamery once stood. It was demolished in 2008 and the new Shelburne Co-operative is now located across the road, seen on the right in the background. The Rosslare to Waterford railway is no longer in use (a section of the line can be seen on the far left of the picture). This is the house of the stationmaster, still standing. (photo: Des Kiely)

The damaged house of stationmaster Paul McCrohan.

importance they attached to disrupting the shipping route.

At the time there was some discussion about the possible protection of Ireland by Britain in a formal defence alliance. German intelligence may have been aware of this and decided to show what Ireland could expect in the event of such an alliance succeeding.

OYLEGATE, 1 January 1941:

Three bombs fell at Oylegate but there was no damage.

BALLYMURN, 3 January 1941:

A German bomber flew in from the coast and soared over the village of The Ballagh. It released ten bombs in a line on the Ballinkeele House estate close to Ballymurn before turning in a circle and disappearing by the same route. The drone of the plane and the explosions were heard for miles around and many families were on their knees saying the rosary.

KILTEALY, 4 January 1941:
Eight bombs were released a few miles north of Kiltealy on the Carlow side of Mount Leinster. They were dropped in a straight line on the mountain slope and one directly hit the Shannon family home near the village of Knockroe in south Carlow. Mary Shannon and daughters

EIRE marking no.16 at Hook Lighthouse, 1940s.
(photo: Irish Military Archive)

Kathleen and Bridget were killed instantly while they slept. Her husband James, their two sons and two grandsons survived the bombing. Again Hitler's government later paid compensation to rebuild the house.

BELFAST, April and May 1941:
The Taoiseach, Éamon de Valera, instructed Dublin Fire Brigade to assist the city in the aftermath of the German bombing blitz that killed over 1,000 people and destroyed half of the houses in Belfast – a gesture much appreciated by the people of Northern Ireland.

DUBLIN, 31 May 1941:
The worst bombing in the South was on the North Strand area of Dublin City, where 34 people were killed, 90 injured and 300 homes were damaged or destroyed. My own mother had just turned 20 and lived a few streets away in Fairview. She often spoke of her memories of the sound of the explosions that night. The German government later expressed regret and promised compensation. This was the last bombing in Ireland by the Luftwaffe during WWII.

Between 1939 and 1945 around 200 aircraft, both Allied and German, came down over neutral Ireland.

On the afternoon of 3 March 1941, in an attack on a British cargo ship, the *Port Townsville*, by two German Heinkel 111 bombers operating out of Brest in Brittany, both aircraft were hit by gunfire from the ship. The *Port Townsville* had just left Newport in South Wales, bound for Australia with a cargo of tin plate. The captain and crew managed to abandon ship but she finally sank the next morning.

One of the planes crash-landed on Lundy Island off Devon, with the crew giving themselves up to the

A Heinkel He 111, the type of bomber that attacked Campile and that crash-landed the following year near Carnsore Point.

lighthouse keeper. The second had lost one engine and its mechanic, Gerhard Rister, had been shot dead while attempting to fix their jammed machine gun. The crew managed to put out a fire in the rear of the aircraft but had to choose between landing in Britain or neutral Ireland, as they had no hope of making it back to their base in France. With black smoke billowing from its tail, its 25-year-old pilot, Lt. Alfred Heinzl, limped the battered aircraft towards Rostoonstown Strand, a broad stretch of beach that separates Lady's Island Lake from the sea.

After several attempts, he managed to land it, with undercarriage up, in soft sand. The surviving crew of four that included Arthur Voigt, Rudolf Hengst and gunner Max Galler, immediately removed Rister's body, machine gun and personal belongings. They walked the short distance to the sand dunes where they set up their machine gun and began firing on the plane, aiming to hit a 250kg bomb it was carrying — similar to that dropped on Campile. When local farmer Nicholas Murphy and

Pilot Alfred Heinzl.

two others approached, the crew warned them to move back into the dunes because they were about to blow up the plane.

Nicholas Redmond, a coastwatch volunteer on duty in Carnsore Look Out Post, had alerted the gardaí and defence forces. A garda from Rosslare was quickly on the scene and witnessed the plane exploding. The crew then broke the machine gun against a rock. Heinzl refused to hand over his revolver and threw it into the lake. The four crewmen were accompanied to Tacumshane village where they were given refreshments by Garrett Murphy and Patrick Keating of Yoletown Farm.

With the arrival of the Defence Forces, the crew surrendered and were marched off and, along with the body of Gerhard Rister, taken to Wexford Military Barracks on Barrack Street. That night they were transferred to the Curragh Internment Camp. Rister was buried with full military honours in Crosstown Cemetery, with a representative of the German Legation present.

At the end of the war, Austrian pilot, Alfred Heinzl, married Kildare girl May Rowan in 1946 and they had two children. He went into business as a commercial artist and was a founder member of the Dublin Gliding Club. Arthur Voigt was repatriated to Germany's Soviet Occupation Zone. He escaped from East Germany in 1949 and returned to Co. Kildare. Voigt and Rudolf Hengst married two sisters and remained living in Ireland.

On 10 June 1941, another Heinkel bomber was shot down by two single-seater RAF Hurricane fighter planes close to the Wexford coast. It crashed into a field, part of the Crosbie family farm at Nethertown, near Carnsore Point. All five crew members were killed and burnt beyond recognition. In an ironic twist, the pilot of one of the Hurricanes, a Frenchman named Roger Motte, had to make a forced landing at Kilmacthomas, Co. Waterford. He was subsequently interned for two years in the Curragh Camp. The German crew were buried with full military honours in Crosstown Cemetery. In 1959 their remains were re-interred in the German Military Cemetery in Glencree, Co. Wicklow. Members of the Soldaten-Kameradschaft, a non-military association, travelled from Bavaria in 2013 to visit the crash site at Nethertown and later the cemetery in Glencree, where they were accompanied by Alfred Heinzl, who laid a wreath on the grave of one of the radio operators killed in the Nethertown crash.

Defence Force and Air Corps personnel at the site of the crashed Luftwaffe plane at Nethertown near Carnsore Point in June 1941. (photo: Military Archives)

BRIDGET AND PADDY HITLER

Dubliner Bridget Dowling fell in love with Adolf Hitler's half-brother Alois Hitler. He was working as a waiter in the Shelbourne Hotel. They eloped to Liverpool and married in London and in 1911 they had a son William Patrick, known as Paddy. But the marriage was short-lived. In 1914 Alois left his wife and 3-year-old son in Liverpool and set off for Germany, where he established a safety-razor business. He married again in Germany despite being still married to Bridget and in 1924 was charged in Germany with bigamy.

Alois Hitler met 17-year-old Bridget Dowling at the Dublin Horse Show in 1909.

When Adolf Hitler became Chancellor in 1933, Paddy travelled to Germany. The pair apparently had a stormy relationship, but Uncle Adolf found Paddy work in the Reichskreditbank in Berlin and he later became a car salesman for Opel. He returned to England in 1938. In early 1939 the newspaper magnate William Randolph Hearst brought Bridget and Paddy to the US for a lecture tour, with Paddy warning America that his uncle was a madman. He joined the US Navy in 1944 and saw action in Europe.

After the war Bridget and Paddy decided to drop out of public view completely and adopted new identities as the Stuart-Houston family and lived on Long Island. In 1947 Patrick married Phyllis, a German woman. Bridget Dowling Hitler died in 1969 and Paddy died in 1987, aged 76. Paddy Hitler's sons Alex, Louis and Brian are Adolf Hitler's last surviving relatives.

Mrs Bridget Hitler, the wife of Adolf Hitler's stepbrother Alois, with her son William Patrick (Paddy) Hitler in New York, 1941.
(photo: Keystone images)

New Ross schoolteacher dismissed for 'living in sin'

Teacher Eileen Flynn and Richie Roche leaving New Ross Courthouse in March 1983, having been sacked from her post after she became pregnant out of marriage. She later appealed unsuccessfully to both the Circuit Court and the High Court. (photo: Irish Times)

EILEEN FLYNN was born in Clonaslee, Rosenallis at the foot of the Slieve Bloom Mountains in Co. Laois in 1955. She pursued a teacher-training course in University College, Galway, and after graduating with an honours degree in 1978, began teaching in a probationary capacity at Holy Faith Secondary School on Thomastown Road in Rosbercon on the outskirts of New Ross. Her high level of teaching skills was noted by the school. She was regarded as a gifted teacher and her position was made permanent in April 1979. The facility was an all-girls Catholic convent school run by the Holy Faith Sisters.

Eileen lived in a flat at 2 Mary Street in the town centre. One day in early 1981, while there was pipe-laying work underway outside on the street, Eileen stepped out and witnessed a little girl walking along one of the pipes fall and badly injure herself. Eileen helped the child to her feet and asked where she lived. The girl took her down the street to her home above a public house on the quay. Her father thanked Eileen for coming to his daughter's assistance.

The business and home of Richie Roche on the quay in New Ross. (photo: Des Kiely)

This was the first time that Eileen met or had ever seen Richie Roche.

Richie was born into the fifty-year-old family business, P. J. Roche public house, a four-storey premises at 7 North Quay, facing the bridge over the River Barrow. He was vice-chair of the local Sinn Féin cumann and in 1980-81 Ireland was gripped by the hunger strikes by Irish republican prisoners in Northern Ireland. Richie was rearing three young children, Regina, Rebecca and Patrick alone, having been deserted by his wife. He kept the pub shut during the day in order to take care of the children and opened at seven o'clock each evening. Eileen began to frequent Roche's and she and Richie eventually fell in love. Their relationship was public knowledge in the town.

The school principal, Sr. Mary Benignus MacDonagh, claimed that parents were starting to complain about the quality of Eileen's work. She said her attendance had become irregular and they were getting further complaints about her 'unacceptable behaviour outside school hours'. She noted after a meeting with Eileen on 13 August 1981 that '…accusations of a serious nature have been made in recent weeks. Many parents are not satisfied to have their children taught by a teacher whose personal life, they claim, is not above reproach…unless there is a remarkable improvement it will lead to the termination of her contract at the end of the school year 1981-82.' Sr. Pauline Leonard suggested that a record of Eileen's behaviour and attendance might be a useful step.

Eileen, who had become very attached to Richie's children, moved in with him in 1981 when in September she discovered she was pregnant. The school was unaware of her pregnancy but continually made her aware they were keeping a file on her. In March 1982, the principal notified Eileen that there were rumours circulating that she was pregnant but Eileen at first denied it, fearing for her job. Two pupils saw Eileen walking through a doorway and noticed her bump and one of the girls told her father, Jack Forristal. He declared that he would not allow his children 'attend a school where an unmarried teacher was having an affair with a married man.' Another parent, Breege Mulally, in a letter of complaint to the nuns, wrote: 'I was worried. I found my children talking about things they should not be talking about at that age.' Some parents went door to door with a petition to have Eileen removed from the school and the following month she was told that a representative of the parents had come to the principal to tell her how they felt about what they were hearing.

Eileen found that she was now being offered fewer teaching hours in the school. She felt under pressure, hounded and harassed and finally admitted she was pregnant and that she was expecting her baby in the summer. Sr. Pauline suggested that she travel to England to stay with her brother, a priest, have the baby there and have it adopted. But Eileen said she had no plans to leave New Ross or to have her baby adopted. There were behind-the-scenes consultations taking place between the nuns and the Bishop of Ferns. The school told her that if she continued in her relationship with a separated man she would be asked to resign or be dismissed. Eileen argued that her private life was separate from her school life.

Our Lady of Lourdes Secondary School in Rosbercon, New Ross, where Eileen Flynn was a teacher from 1978 until her dismissal in 1982. (photo: Des Kiely)

She continued to teach up to the last day of term before the summer break, 4 June 1982. Four days later she gave birth to baby Richard at Wexford General Hospital. In early August, the school summoned her to a meeting with the manager of the Holy Faith schools in Ireland, Sr. Mary Anna Power. She was asked again to resign but refused. In a follow-up letter she was told that she was being dismissed '...because your conduct has been fundamentally inconsistent with your position as a teacher in the school...and in the interests of the pupils I would be glad if you would not attend the school when it reopens...' She was given four months' pay of £2,026 and told not to return to the school in September.

On 29 August Eileen told the principal that, on the advice of her solicitor, she would contest the manager's decision and on the 28 February 1983, notice of claim under the provisions of the Unfair Dismissals Act, 1977, which prohibits pregnancy discrimination, was served. Her solicitor, Simon Kennedy, expected she would win her case on the grounds that she was dismissed because she was pregnant.

Eileen sought to be reinstated in her post but lost her unfair dismissal case at the Employment Appeals Tribunal. Bank of Ireland refused to handle an appeal fund that was set up to help her fight her dismissal. She appealed to the Circuit Court, where Judge Noel Ryan upheld the tribunal's verdict. Dismissing her appeal, he famously claimed that the nuns had been too lenient with her. 'Elsewhere in the world, women were condemned to death for this sort of offence,' he said. The case became a story of great national interest and Eileen Flynn became a rallying point in the 1980s for people who believed that the Catholic Church needed to be challenged on their stance within Irish society.

Summonses for attendance at court were issued against Bishop Laurence Forrestal, the then Bishop of Ossory; the Archbishop of Dublin Dr. Dermot Ryan and the Archbishop of Armagh Cardinal Tomás Ó Fiaich. Only the local bishop attended. She finally lost her appeal to the High Court on 8 March 1985. In his reserved judgement, Justice Declan Costello said: 'I do not think that the respondents over-emphasise the power of example on the lives of the pupils in the school and they were entitled to conclude that the appellant's conduct was capable of damaging their efforts to foster in their pupils' norms of behaviour and religious tenets which the school had been established to

Eileen Flynn (1955-2008) was a victim of the 1980s, a time that could be a dark place for women in Ireland. (photo: Irish Times)

promote.' Eileen said that she could not afford the legal costs to appeal further to the Supreme Court or the European Court of Justice.

In the years that followed, Eileen never once regretted her decision because she believed that 'she stuck with the truth', said Simon Kennedy, her solicitor, who was a former seminarian. 'Her case would cause a scandal and it had to be gotten rid of. That is how the Catholic Church viewed it and how they handled such matters. Eileen never wanted to cause controversy nor did she want publicity.' Kennedy received several death threats for taking the case on, Eileen became the target of abusive phone calls and her mother in Co. Laois became the object of ridicule. For fear of breaching Section 31 of the Broadcasting Act, RTÉ would not interview Richie Roche, who was a Sinn Féin activist, but Eileen was not. The case was the subject of much media comment and public controversy in the period and it caused a polarization of opinion in Ireland at the time, of both outrage and agreement. Enniscorthy writer Colm Tóibín described the reports on the Gay Byrne Show on RTÉ radio as reminiscent of a Thomas Hardy novel.

Writing to *The Irish Times* in 1995, Sr. Rosemary Duffy, the principal of the Holy Faith Order wrote: 'Eileen Flynn was dismissed because in the town where most of the pupils and parents of the school lived she openly and despite warnings to the contrary continued to live a lifestyle flagrantly in conflict with the norms which the school sought to promote.' Sr. Anna said 'she just flaunted it and did not try to hide it or redeem herself.'

The first divorce referendum in 1986 was defeated but the subsequent referendum of November 1995 was carried by 51 per cent to 49. Legislation followed in June 1996 and Eileen married Richie Roche on 8 September 1997 in a civil ceremony, as she was no longer a practising Catholic. They were now a family of seven, including two children of their own, Richie and Diarmuid, and they ran two pubs together.

The Holy Faith Sisters withdrew from Rosbercon in 1998 when the first lay principal was appointed and the school is now known as Our Lady of Lourdes secondary school. Eileen missed teaching and thought she was unemployable because of the case. 'It ended my teaching career,' she later said in an interview in the *Irish Independent*. 'I'm too long out of it. I accept I was a scapegoat but I have no time for bitterness, you just get on with your life. That's not to say you don't think it's wrong.' But she was finally offered a teaching post in 2005 by the principal of the local CBS Primary School, Brian McMahon, and in 2007 her position was made permanent.

On the night of 9 September 2008, the day after her 11th wedding anniversary, Eileen was out with friends in the Three Bullet Gate Bar in New Ross. She stepped outside for a cigarette and collapsed and died. She was aged just 53. Simon Kennedy, her solicitor, said that Richie and her family were devastated at the suddenness of her death. 'She left her mark in this town; she left her mark on all of us. Most especially, she left her mark on her family. Perhaps the truth is you end up where your heart is and that's the bottom line. Eileen ended her days with the man and family she loved and back at a job she adored – teaching.' She was laid to rest in the cemetery grounds of the Church of the Assumption in Rosbercon, next to the school that she was dismissed from twenty-six years earlier.

The obscene irony of the time was not lost on many following Eileen's death. While she was being sacked for 'living in sin' with a separated man and having his child, just a short distance away in Fethard-on-Sea, Fr. Seán Fortune from Gorey was continuing to rape teenage boys with impunity. Fortune was educated at St. Peter's College in Wexford and in 1999 committed suicide in New Ross while awaiting trial for 66 charges of sexual abuse against 29 boys. Donal Herlihy was the Bishop of Ferns at the time of Eileen Flynn's dismissal and was criticized in the Ferns Report in 2005 for describing sexual behaviour towards boys as 'moral failure'. His successor was Brendan Comiskey, who resigned in 2002 following the transmission of the BBC documentary *Suing the Pope*, alleging that he did not report allegations against Fortune.

'Monster from the deep' stranded at Wexford Harbour

ON THE MORNING of 25 March 1891, 20-year-old Edward 'Ned' Wickham spotted an enormous creature struggling to get back out to deep water having been stranded on Swanton's Bank, a sandbar close to the Hantoon Channel east of Rosslare Point and near the mouth of Wexford Harbour.

Ned was a lifeboat pilot and son of Rosslare Fort lifeboat coxswain Thomas Wickham. The Wickhams lived in the small village that had grown up around the Fort, which was sited at Rosslare Point at the tip of Rosslare sandspit.

Ned Wickham rowed out with lifeboat colleagues to view the unusual visitor and continued to observe the animal from a safe distance. By the next day its struggles had become weaker. Ned was upset and tried to put the giant mammal out of its misery, beating it with an iron bar in an attempt to kill the creature. He finally killed it by plunging a makeshift harpoon into its body below one of the flippers.

The newspapers of the day reported the arrival of the 'strange visitant from strange seas' and sightseers came from far and wide to observe the body

Rosslare Fort lifeboat coxswain Ned Wickham pictured twenty years later in 1911.

from Rosslare Point and took boat trips out to witness the 'monster from the deep' from close up.

Initially wrongly identified as a sperm whale, which is a toothed whale, the 'monster' turned out to be an 82-foot (25-metre) young female blue whale, which has baleen (used in corset making) rather than teeth. The blue whale is the largest animal known to have ever lived. It had migrated up the east coast and got caught by the low tide.

A cutting from the *Liverpool Mercury* on 30 March 1891 reads: 'Several whales have latterly been reported as having been seen off the Irish coast, and on Saturday the death of one 100ft long is reported from Wexford. On Thursday, a fisherman named Wickham, being at the entrance to the harbour, saw an unusual disturbance of the sea a short distance out. He plainly discerned the back and tail of an enormous creature who was evidently struggling to get out into deep water. The pilots at the Fort station put out in a boat, but were cautious not to approach too close to the unusual visitor. They continued to watch, and on Friday, its struggles becoming weaker, Wickham ventured to approach the monster, and succeeded in plunging a long knife into the body of the creature under one of the fins. It turned out to be a whale about 100ft long by 60ft girth.'

WHALES ON THE IRISH COAST.

Several whales have latterly been reported as having been seen off the Irish coast, and on Saturday the death of one 100ft. long is reported from Wexford. On Thursday, a fisherman named Wickham, being at the entrance to the harbour, saw an unusual disturbance of the sea a short distance out. He plainly discerned the back and tail of an enormous creature who was evidently struggling to get out into deep water. The pilots at the Fort station put out in a boat, but were cautious not to approach too close to the unusual visitor. They continued to watch, and on Friday, its struggles becoming weaker, Wickham ventured to approach the monster, and succeeded in plunging a long knife into the body of the creature under one of the fins. It turned out to be a whale about 100ft. long by 60ft. girth.

The Receiver of Wreck, an agent of the Crown, advertised the mammal's 4,500-kilo carcass for auction in *The Freeman's Journal*. It was purchased for £111 (about €15,000 in today's terms) by the Wexford merchant William Armstrong, who had a business on the Main Street and was Chairman of the Harbour Commissioners. Ned was awarded £50 (the equivalent of about €7,000 today) by the Receiver of Wreck. Normally only one-third of the salvage money realized was granted but in this case the authorities believed that Ned was deserving of more considering his brave efforts.

Wexford merchant William Armstrong purchased the whale's carcass and sold it to London's Natural History Museum.

'This should keep the pilots on the look-out for another whale' suggested one of the local newspapers.

The whale's oil, obtained from its blubber, was collected and its lean meat sold as pet food. The 630 gallons of oil alone made Armstrong about €7,000 in today's money. The carcass was cut up at Raven Point and sold to the Natural History Museum in London for £256 (about €35,000), making a handsome profit. It arrived at the museum later that year.

The skeleton was kept in storage for over 40 years until it first went on display in 1934 in the specially constructed Mammals Hall, where it was

The skeleton, the largest specimen in the Natural History Museum in London, being hoisted into position in the purpose-built Mammals Hall in 1934. (photo: Natural History Museum London)

The Wexford whale, now named 'Hope', has been moved to the Hintze Hall in London's Natural History Museum and is currently the building's centrepiece. (photo: Natural History Museum London)

suspended from the rafters above a 28.6-metre life-size model.

Over 80 years later, in 2017, the gigantic 4.5-tonne skeleton was moved to the heart of the museum in a project lasting almost two years. Its deconstruction and rebuilding was the biggest ever project undertaken by the museum, requiring many hands and a range of expertise. The skeleton had to be cleaned and conserved before it was laser-scanned and a 3D-model was created for scientific posterity. It took more than six months to complete the full 3D rendering of the skeleton.

The blue whale replaced 'Dippy' the diplodocus dinosaur, a plaster-cast replica skeleton, after 112 years as the museum's best-known prize exhibit in the Hintze Hall, the largest public gallery in the museum.

The Wexford whale, now hanging in a dramatic dive position, has been named 'Hope' by the museum as a symbol of humanity's power to shape a sustainable future. The museum's centrepiece was unveiled by its patron Kate Middleton, Duchess of Cambridge, and the conservationist David Attenborough in July 2017.

In the 1800s there were an estimated 250,000 blue whales inhabiting the world's oceans but commercial whaling in the 1800s and early 1900s drove the animal to the brink of extinction. In 1966, when the population was down to around 400, the world took the decision to legally protect blue whales from commercial hunting. There are now between 10,000 and 25,000 in the world.

14 killed in Bunclody over the forced sale of two heifers

Ryland Road, Newtownbarry (Bunclody), scene of the killings in 1831. (photo: National Library of Ireland)

WHAT BECAME known as the 'Battle of the Pound' or the 'Newtownbarry Massacre' took place on 18 June 1831 in Bunclody (then named Newtownbarry) in the early days of the Tithe War.

Bunclody lies on the Wexford-Carlow border, where the River Clody meets the River Slaney. In 1719 the lands around the town were acquired by James Barry, who renamed it Newtownbarry. The Barry name is believed to have come to Ireland with Philip de Barri who arrived from Glamorgan in South Wales as part of the Anglo-Norman invasion and was granted lands in County Cork. In 1950, a plebiscite held by Wexford County Council offered the town's ratepayers the opportunity to change the name back to Bunclody. The vote was carried and it reverted to the old name by Government order, signed on 11 November 1950.

In 1542, Henry VIII was granted the title 'King of Ireland' and head of the 'Church in Ireland'. However, three-quarters of the population remained members of the Catholic Church. Tithes were payable for the upkeep of the Church of Ireland clergy and their properties while the Catholic Church depended on voluntary contributions. It was not until 1869 that the tax was abolished, when the Church of Ireland was disestablished by the Gladstone government's Church Disestablishment Act.

The enforcement of tithes was bitterly resented by Catholics and also by Presbyterians, who were mainly located in Ulster. About six million Catholics were being forced to pay the tithes for churches to which they did not belong. Many of the clergy had no congregation and some even lived elsewhere. It was claimed that Church of Ireland clergy were paid much more than their counterparts in England. Several rectors sold their interests in the tithes to wealthy farmers, some Catholic, known as 'tithe farmers'.

With the passing of the Catholic Emancipation Act in 1829, the obligation to pay tithes to the Church of Ireland remained. This led to an organized campaign of resistance to the payment that became known as the Tithe War. The war was more a civil dispute, even though people died on both sides.

The Tithe War of 1831-36 was a reaction to the enforcement of the payment of one-tenth of annual produce or earnings by farmers, including tenant farmers, to the Church of Ireland, the so-called established church. Irrespective of an individual's religious adherence, the tax was compulsory. It was often paid in the form of produce or livestock rather than in cash. The tithe collectors or proctors were some of the most despised men in every county. They travelled the country collecting the tax from many who could not afford it and who were already contributing to the local Catholic Church. If the money was not forthcoming they seized furniture, beds, blankets, kettles or anything else they could lay their hands on.

This pig refuses to hand over 10% of her litter to a Protestant clergyman.

There was almost daily conflict as the military and police were constantly called out to support the collectors in making their seizures. In 1830, a movement against the payment of tithes began, mainly in the south of Ireland in the counties of Kilkenny and Wexford. Men would arrive at public meetings brandishing hurling sticks, vowing to no longer pay the tithes.

GRAIGUENAMANAGH

The first clash was on 3 March 1831 in Graiguenamanagh, Co. Kilkenny. With the blessing of his bishop, a Catholic priest arranged for his farmer parishioners to transfer their cattle into his name before selling them and so avoid seizure by the tithe proctors. A force of 120 yeomen (members of the mainly Protestant militia) tried to take possession of the livestock but left with none.

The success of this confrontation emboldened the farmers who were resisting payment. They had the Catholic Church on their side with Dr. James Doyle, the Bishop of Kildare and Leighlin and a native of New Ross, describing the tax as 'unjust in principle, destructive of religion, and subversive of the peace and happiness of our native land.' A letter from him was used by the movement as a call to resist:

> 'There are many noble traits in the Irish character, mixed with failings which have always raised obstacles to their own well-being; but an innate love of justice, and an indomitable hatred of oppression, is like a gem upon the front of our nation which no darkness can obscure. To this fine quality I trace their hatred of tithes; may it be as lasting as their love of justice!'

NEWTOWNBARRY

The incident in Newtownbarry was one of the worst during the Tithe War. Two local farmers named Doyle and Nowlan complained that their tithes were being demanded even before they were due. Rev. Alexander McClintock, with the support of his bishop, had two heifers, worth less than £3, seized from the farmers and moved to the pound on Ryland Road, the main road into the town from the Enniscorthy side. They were to be sold at an auction in the town on Saturday 18 June 1831.

The sale was strongly opposed locally and people vowed to disrupt it. Posters appeared throughout counties Wexford, Carlow and even Wicklow with the wording: 'Attend to an auction of your neighbours' cattle on Saturday next, the 18th inst., seized for tithe by the Rev. Alexander McClintock.' Trouble was anticipated by the local magistrate, Captain William Graham, who ordered upwards of 200 yeomen and 37 policemen from Myshall, Scarawalsh and Enniscorthy to be on standby on the day of the sale.

A large crowd, including the cattlemen Doyle and Nowlan, gathered at the pound and they got noisier as the militia drew closer. Scuffles broke out as some in the crowd began to throw stones. When Captain Graham arrived he ordered them to disperse. The cattle managed to break loose and when their owners attempted to reclaim them, Captain Graham ordered the yeomen to open fire on the crowd. They shot three people dead and the throng ran for cover through open ground towards the River Slaney. They refused to cease firing even when ordered to and a yeoman, William Rogan, was accidentally killed by a musket shot to the head from one of his own men. When the shooting finally stopped, a total of 14 lay dead or dying and a further 25 were wounded. The police had not fired on the day, which demonstrated the sectarian aspect to the killings. The incident became known as Black Saturday or the 'Battle of the Pound'.

The bodies of those killed were laid out in the Sunday School opposite the courthouse on Church Street, where an inquest on the victims was held over the next few days. The jury of twelve consisted of six Catholics and six Protestants. The Catholic jurymen wanted to name certain yeomen who were believed to have fired without the command of Captain Graham. The Protestant jurymen said the victims were killed by persons unknown from the yeomanry and police. In the end justice did not prevail and nobody was ever prosecuted for the murders.

CARRICKSHOCK

Worse slaughter was to follow on 14 December 1831 in the townland of Carrickshock, near Knocktopher in south Kilkenny. A tithe collector named Edmund Butler was under the protection of a party of 38 armed policemen on horseback. They were commanded by the chief constable, Captain Gibbons. A crowd of 500 people were following and demanding that Butler be handed over to them. 'Give us Butler!' they shouted continually. An attempt was made to force Butler to eat the summonses that he was carrying. They found themselves in a tight laneway with high walls on either side. When Butler was hit over the head with a large stone, Gibbons ordered his men to fire but they were caught in too tight a space. The protesters began removing large rocks from the wall and heaving them down on the police. Gibbons, 14 of his men and Butler were stoned to death or killed with pitchforks, clubs and hurling sticks. Between 25 and 30 people in the crowd also died.

The Battle at Carrickshock, Co. Kilkenny (from Cassell's Illustrated History of England, 1895)

In July of the following year in nearby Ballyhale an enormous crowd, estimated to have been about 200,000, gathered in support of those charged as a result of the Battle of Carrickshock. People travelled from four counties by horse and cart and on foot. It was the largest peaceful gathering of people in the country. The crowd was addressed by the barrister and liberator Daniel O'Connell. Those arrested after Carrickshock were defended by O'Connell and were all exonerated, mainly because nobody, apart from the surviving policemen, would give evidence.

There were more clashes over the next four years, most notably on 18 December 1834 in north County Cork. The Rathcormac Massacre (also known as the Gortroe Massacre) took place in the parish of Gortroe near the village of Rathcormac. In an attempt to enforce a mere 40-shilling payment for Archdeacon Ryder, a small number of police constables reinforced by 200 troops resulted in the deaths of up to twenty residents of the village when the military opened fire on the crowd who were blocking them.

The mayhem continued over the next two years and the police were being stretched to such an extent that the government suspended collections of tithes. It was said that 'It cost a shilling to collect tuppence.' In 1838, partial relief from the tax was granted by the Tithe Commutation Act, and with the Church Disestablishment Act of 1869 the tithe system was abolished for ever.

Living with the ghosts of a medieval house near Fethard

Eileen Cloney outside her home, Dungulph Castle. (photo: Des Kiely)

EILEEN CLONEY lives in Dungulph Castle, 3km north of Fethard-on-Sea, a fortified three-storey dwelling built about 500 years ago. The original property, probably constructed of timber, dated from 1330. The house retains many of its original features and in the north-east corner is a spiral stairway tower. The castle was restored one hundred years ago by Eileen's grandfather Michael Cloney. It has had only four family owners in its seven centuries of remarkable history: the Whitty, Loftus, Devereux and Cloney families. It is one of the few medieval castles still in private hands in the country.

WHITTY FAMILY

The site is believed to have been held by the heirs of John de Villiers, a member of the Knights Templar, the powerful Christian military order during the time of the Crusades. The Knights were granted lands by Henry II at

Templetown on the Hook Peninsula in 1172 to protect the eastern side on Waterford Harbour. According to a plaque at the entrance to Dungulph Castle, the original house was built in 1330 by the Whitty family of Ballyteigue, near Kilmore, who owned 400 acres of surrounding land. During the Confederate Wars (1641-53), a party of 16 Royalist troops, under the command of Lieutenant Treviscoe, laid siege to the castle in 1642. All were killed in an ambush by Confederate soldiers led by Captain Thomas Rossiter and buried in a nearby field. The castle was then in the possession of Walter Whitty.

LOFTUS FAMILY

Following the Cromwellian conquest of Ireland in 1649, Dungulph Castle and its lands were confiscated and granted to Captain Betts (Bates). In 1654, it was purchased by Nicholas Loftus, who took up residence in Fethard Castle and died there in 1666. His brother Henry occupied Dungulph and in the late 1670s moved to Redmond Hall, which he renamed Loftus Hall. Henry Loftus died in 1716 and was succeeded by his son, another Nicholas. In 1720

Henry Loftus (1636-1716), who occupied Dungulph Castle before moving to Redmond Hall, later renamed Loftus Hall.

when Eleanor, daughter of Nicholas married, Dungulph Castle passed to her husband John Cliffe. Another daughter of Loftus of Fethard Castle, Eleanor Mildway, married John Lynn of Fethard and they later occupied Dungulph.

DEVEREUX FAMILY

The Devereux family succeeded the Lynns in Dungulph around 1790. The castle was now in the hands of John (known locally as Seán Rua) and Mary Devereux at the time of the 1798 rebellion. Two of their sons had taken part in the Battle of Ross in 1798 and when troops from Duncannon

Eleanor Loftus Lynn (1783-1846), granddaughter of Eleanor Loftus Mildway, was born in Dungulph.

Eileen Cloney's impression of how the dwelling next to the castle looked between 1800 and 1900.

Fort called looking for them and could not find them, they set fire to the castle and mill. Neighbours helped save the mill, having put out the fire with the abundance of water in the mill-pond but the castle was destroyed, with only the outer walls surviving. To escape execution, both sons fled to America. The Devereux family converted an outbuilding into a two-storey dwelling, which they continued to occupy. The shell of the castle was used for milling and keeping livestock.

CLONEY FAMILY

After the Battle of Ross, the 24-year-old rebel leader Thomas Cloney of Moneyhore near Enniscorthy, was given shelter in Old Ross by his cousin Martin Cloney, who held a lease on a small mill farm near the village. Old Ross had a German Protestant population that had fled their Palatine homeland in 1709 and the Cloneys were a Catholic family, a minority amongst them. An estimated 2,000 rebels had lost their lives in the Battle of Ross and, in retaliation, between 100 and 200 Protestants were shot, piked and burnt to death in the Scullabogue barn massacre at the foot of Carrickbyrne Hill. The Protestant church of St. Mary's in Old Ross was burnt to the ground — the only one to be set alight during the rebellion.

A son of Martin Cloney of Old Ross, Thomas, married Eleanor Devereux of Dungulph Castle in 1817 and ownership of the castle then transferred to Thomas. They had nine children and Thomas, along with his father-in-law, John Devereux, managed the farm and mill. When Thomas died in 1869, aged 81, his son Garrett took over the farming and milling.

There were two other mills in the townland of Dungulph, one north-west of the castle and the other, a disused watermill, can be seen off the road towards Poulfur. This watermill would have been engaged in grinding wheat into flour for baking bread but also as a flax mill; processing flax for spinning yarn. To the north-east of the castle is the site of a windmill, possibly similar to that in Tacumshane, that would have produced animal feed from grinding barley and oats. The Dungulph windmill was operated by Garrett's brother Martin, and when he died in 1878 it became disused and was demolished around the end of the 19th century.

Another son, John, and his sister Mary ran a general store in New Ross. When Garrett died aged 56 in 1888, they sold the shop and John managed the mill and farm. Their sisters, Margaret (Molly) and Bridget, both married but were childless. On losing their husbands, they sold their respective farms in Camross and Duncannon and moved back home to Dungulph, sharing the house with John and Mary. When John died in 1896, aged 77, the three sisters needed someone to take his place. They offered the position to their cousin Michael Cloney of Old Ross.

Aged 30 and working as a clerk in a shop in Dublin, Michael accepted their offer. When he moved in, he embarked on modernizing and extending the mill and corn-drying kilns, and constructing large stables and other farm buildings. In 1904, he used the stones from the ruined windmill to build a lofted stable.

Michael Cloney and his mother Johanna from Old Ross. Michael undertook the complete renovation of the ruined Dungulph Castle in the early 1900s.

By 1909, all three elderly sisters had passed away.

Michael, still a bachelor, bought out Dungulph Castle from the Land Commission and spent a considerable amount of money on his main project — the restoration work on Dungulph Castle, turning it back into a house; it had lain 100 years in ruin. This was complete by 1917 when he married Elizabeth Murphy of Kilmokea, who sadly died from tetanus within a few months of their wedding.

Michael was a founder member of the Shelburne Co-operative Society in Campile, becoming its first chairman in 1919. In 1925, now aged 59, he

The Cloney household at Dungulph Castle, c.1900.
Back: Michael with his cousins Margaret (Molly) and Mary.
Front: Mary ('Mother Peter') and Bridget.

married Ellen Cavanagh from the Ballygarrett area and they had one son, Seán. Michael was very active in local politics and was appointed Peace Commissioner by the Free State authorities following Partition in 1921. He served on many county boards until his death in 1935, when Seán was just seven. Seán attended Rockwell College boarding school in Co. Tipperary from the age of 14 but he had to give up his education after just two years to help his mother Ellen run the farm. She died two years later in 1943. The watermill, on the Dungulph stream, continued to produce oatmeal for use in porridge, until the early 1950s.

FETHARD-ON-SEA BOYCOTT

Seán married local girl Sheila Kelly in 1949. The Kellys were Protestant cattle dealers in nearby Fethard-on-Sea. Both aged 22, they eloped to London, where they married. Their first two daughters, Eileen and Mary, were born in 1951 and 1953 respectively.

Sheila's intention was to raise their children in both traditions and while Seán attended Mass in Poulfur, Sheila attended St. Mogue's in Fethard where she was an active member.

Catholics who married non-Catholics, under the 1908 Catholic *'Ne Temere'* decree, were obliged to have all children of the marriage baptized and reared as Catholics. Before then, the tradition was for boys to be raised in their father's religion and girls in their mother's. Despite protests from Sheila, the nuns in the Catholic nursing home where Eileen and later Mary were born, had them both immediately baptized. Although the Catholic Church did not recognize Church of Ireland baptisms, the Church of Ireland did recognize Catholic ones. This meant that the girls could not be baptized again in the Church of Ireland.

In 1957, Eileen was nearing her sixth birthday. Seán was coming under pressure to send his daughter to the Catholic school in Poulfur. But Sheila was determined that she attend the Church of Ireland school. The pressure became so much for Sheila that she took the girls to Scotland, where they remained for over seven months. Back home in the local Catholic church in Poulfur, the parish priest called on all Catholics in the area to boycott Protestants and their businesses until the 'kidnapped' children were returned. The four-month-long boycott throughout the summer of 1957 became a national and international sensation, known as the 'Fethard-on-Sea Boycott'. Under pressure from the Taoiseach, Éamon de Valera, the boycott was finally called off in September.

Seán and Sheila Cloney pictured in Trafalgar Square, London on their wedding day, 8 October 1949.

Eileen with younger sister Mary at Dungulph Castle in 1957, the year of the 'Fethard-on-Sea Boycott'.

Sheila returned with the two girls on New Year's Eve and they were both home-schooled. Seán and Sheila's third child, Hazel, was born in 1961, baptized in both churches and attended the local Catholic school.

The Catholic Church had been forced to call off the boycott before the Cloney children had returned to Fethard. The Protestant Church in Ireland was badly damaged by the *'Ne Temere'* decree; fewer children were attending church, resulting in reduced income for parishes and Protestant-run schools including the school in Fethard were forced to close. The restoration of friendly relations came slowly to the people of the village. The boycott had caused a serious split which had a long-lasting effect and was the subject of the 1999 feature film *A Love Divided.*

In later years, Seán took a great interest in local history and in particular in the family history of the Colcloughs of Tintern Abbey, where he conducted guided tours. He was an active member of the Wexford Historical Society.

In 1995, he was involved in a serious car accident at Ferrycarrig and was wheelchair-bound until his death in 1999, aged 73. Mary, aged only 44, died a year previously. Sheila passed away in 2009, aged 83. Eileen continues to live and farm at Dungulph Castle and is also a fine artist. She has converted part of the lofted stable, built by her grandfather Michael, into an art studio.

Artist Eileen Cloney at work in her studio at Dungulph Castle. (photo: Des Kiely)

North and South Slobs: Wexford's Dutch-like landscape

View from the North Slob seawall or dyke, taken at high tide. The reclaimed land here is up to 3 metres below sea level, the lowest point in Ireland. (photo: Des Kiely)

POLDERS, canals, dykes and pump stations, reminiscent of a Dutch landscape, make up the North and South Slobs of Wexford Harbour. In school we learned that the highest point in Ireland is Carrauntoohil at 1,038 metres but did you know that the lowest point in the country is the North Slob, lying up to 3 metres (10 feet) below sea level? The word slab (pronounced 'slob') means 'mud' in Irish and 'mire' in Danish. The name Wexford comes from the Viking name 'Waesfjord' meaning the 'Bay of the Mudflats'.

Wexford Harbour comprised thousands of acres of mudflats and sandbanks. Begerin Island was one of several small islands that protruded above the mudflats of what is now the North Slob. In the 5th century, St. Ibar established a monastery there and in the 13th century the Benedictines built a church on the site.

In 1814, the Thomas brothers from England made the first attempt at reclaiming mudflats or slobs in Wexford Harbour for the landowner, James Boyd of Rosslare House. They hoped to recover 800 acres in the southern area of the harbour and built a sea embankment but just as the work was completed, it was breached during a strong gale. Only 200 acres were salvaged.

The remnants of the bank can still be seen today at low tide. With the passing of an Act of Parliament in 1840, which offered government aid toward the reclamation of waste land in Ireland, a further plan was proposed by a Scottish syndicate. They wanted to reclaim extensive acreage in both the north and south parts of the harbour, as well as at Our Lady's Island, Ballyteigue and Bannow. But the Wexford Harbour proposal was opposed by many local landowners and shipping merchants, who foresaw problems for vessels using the harbour as it might silt up even further.

John E. Redmond (1806-65) was a member of the family that dominated business and political life in Wexford in the 19th century. He was a banker and magistrate and became a Liberal MP for Wexford in 1859. His nephew William was elected Home Rule Party MP in 1872 and William's son John, born in 1856, became leader of the the Irish Parliamentary Party in 1900.

John E. Redmond was behind the development and extension of the quay to the south and the construction of an embankment in the 1830s as far as Fisher's Row. He created a jetty for steamships and a dockyard for shipbuilding, Wexford's first major industry. Redmond also helped bring the railway to the town in the 1860s and 70s. A group headed up by Redmond began work on the North Slob embankment in 1847, despite objections

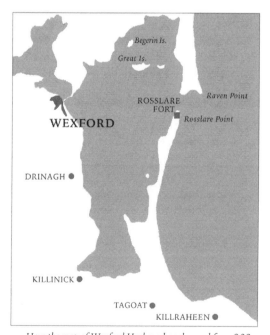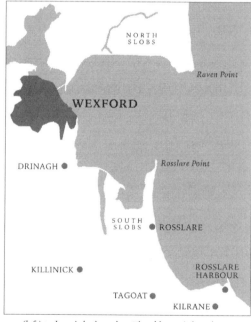

How the map of Wexford Harbour has changed from 200 years ago (left) to how it looks today. The old map is based on an 1811 map of Co. Wexford by Valentine Gill, a surveyor from Enniscorthy. © Des Kiely

The North Slob seawall, built between 1847-49.

echoing those that had gone before. He had to obtain and Act of Parliament to proceed with the project. The construction gave much-needed employment at the height of the Famine, with labourers travelling from all over the county carrying shovels and picks. Over 2,400 acres of land were rendered arable by digging out canals and drains and a pumping station built to remove excess water. The seawall or dyke, built across the northern side of Wexford Harbour, was eight feet wide and the whole project was completed in two years. Much of the new fertile land dried out and was ready to be ploughed and cultivated by the following year. With an improvement in drainage over the past fifty years, high-grade cereals are now planted.

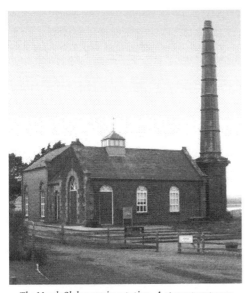

The North Slob pumping station. A steam pump was originally installed in the pump house. The present electric one can pump out 64 tons of water per minute.
(photo: Lucy Kiely)

Work began on the South Slob embankment in 1854, incorporating the remains of the first attempt by the Thomas brothers forty years earlier. The pumping station and South Slob Boundary Canal were completed in 1857. But the company behind its construction went bankrupt in 1870 because the soil failed to harden. The land was sold on but happily the ground finally solidified for the new owners. Many breaches occurred in the embankment, with the last collapse happening in 1935.

The South Slob comprises a 1,400-acre farm – one of Ireland's largest – 400 acres of forestry and 250 acres of waterways. Along with the North Slob, it forms part of the larger Wexford Slobs and Harbour Special Protection Area for birds, part of the EU's Natura 2000 network.

The reclamation of the slobs lessened the flow of water into Wexford Harbour, reducing the size of the port considerably. This contributed to further silting-up and a build-up of the bar at the entrance, as had been predicted by some. With sailing ships being replaced by bigger steamships in the 19th century, Wexford Harbour suffered a huge decline and much of the maritime activity began moving to the new harbour further south near Greenore. Named Rosslare Harbour, the port was developed by the Great Southern

The South Slob pump-house
photographed in 1947.
(photo: Caoimhín Ó Danachair/Dúchas)

The pump-house, built in 1857, has been
pumping water continuously from the
reclaimed mudflats into the South Slob
Boundary Canal for over 150 years.
(photo: Des Kiely)

and Western Railway with the construction of a pier and the opening of a train station in 1906, and a ferry link to the newly-built Fishguard Harbour.

The tides and currents of the Slaney frequently shift mud and sand, and islands of sand can appear and then disappear over the course of just a few weeks. Although Wexford Harbour is no longer suitable for large ships, by transplanting seed mussel to the mudflats a vibrant mussel industry has been established and large mussel dredgers now line the quays.

The Redmond Memorial was built in 1867 to commemorate John E. Redmond who died two years earlier and had instigated the reclamation of lands including the ground where Redmond Square itself stands.

The North Slob began to attract wildfowl, leading to the establishment of the Wexford Wildfowl Reserve. The original 270 acres of reserve lands were purchased in 1968 by the Department of Lands and the Irish Wildbird Conservancy, with additional funding provided by the World Wildlife Fund and Guinness Breweries. It was officially opened in 1974 and over 200 acres were added in 1990. A further 50 acres were purchased in 2003, bringing the total area up to its present 550 acres. Currently as many as 10,000 Greenland white-fronted geese, one-third of the world population, migrate from Western Greenland via Iceland to spend the winters in the North Slob.

The Redmonds continued to be involved in reclamation around Wexford Harbour. Further land was recovered from the Slaney north of the bridge towards Carcur by 1870. Near the junction of Selskar Street and Slaney Street, an old seawall was removed and the area known as Redmond Place (now Redmond Square) was created. A further embankment was built along the edge of the harbour to carry the new railway and the town's first train station was built here in 1874. Two years after his death in 1865, John E. Redmond was honoured by the erection of an obelisk in the centre of Redmond Square.

Aer Lingus Flight 712 crash: was there a cover-up?

Wreckage from the fatal crash near Tuskar Rock being landed at Rosslare Harbour four months later, July 1968.
(photo: Getty Images)

IN ITS over 80-year history, Aer Lingus have had a relatively good safety record. Founded in 1936, they have had three fatal accidents. In 1952, a Douglas DC-3 (an ex-military Dakota), en route from London to Dublin, crashed in Snowdonia, Wales, killing all 20 passengers and 3 crew on board.

The British-built Vickers Viscount came into service in 1953, when BEA began regular passenger flights on the world's first scheduled turboprop airline service. The Viscount was popular with both operators and passengers. However, because of its complexity and revolutionary design, it needed meticulous maintenance. Of the 445 built, over 150 were involved in accidents worldwide, 144 of these resulting total loss of the aircraft – one-third of the total fleet. Up to the end of 1995, Viscount crashes had caused 1,740 deaths – a shocking safety record. Aer Lingus operated approximately 20 Viscount aircraft in the 1950s and 1960s and lost three within nine months between June 1967 and March 1968.

In June 1967, a Viscount on a pilot-training flight stalled and spun to the ground near Asbourne, Co. Meath, killing all 3 crew on board. Three months later, in September 1967, another Viscount crash-landed at Bristol. There were no fatalities but the plane was damaged beyond repair. However, the crash off the Wexford coast in March 1968, involving yet another Viscount, was Ireland's worst air disaster. Following the crash, Aer Lingus put their remaining eleven Viscounts up for sale, replacing them with Boeings. Sales of refurbished Viscounts worldwide, mostly to African operators, continued into the 1990s and it is thought that the last Viscount to fly left service in about 2008.

This Viscount 803, later named 'St. Phelim', was purchased by the Dutch airline KLM in 1957. It was sold to Aer Lingus in 1966 and re-registered as EI-AOM. On 13 March 1968, eleven days before the fatal crash, the 'St. Phelim' was departing Birmingham for a flight to Cork. Just before take-off, it returned to the terminal building, where maintenance staff spent an hour working on the wing. Finally taking off, it was a rough ride with loud noises every time the plane climbed.

Flight EI 712, 'St. Phelim', left Cork Airport at 11.32am on Sunday morning 24 March 1968 in clear weather, bound for London Heathrow Airport. At 11.38, when the aircraft had passed through 7,000 feet, clearance on course towards Tuskar was given by Shannon Air Traffic Control. At 11.40, after the flight had reported it was over Youghal at 7,500 feet climbing to 17,000 feet, Air Traffic Control suggested that, if desired, the flight could route directly to Strumble Head in Pembrokeshire, west of Fishguard. No direct

The Aer Lingus Viscount 803, 'St. Phelim', registration number EI-AOM, on taxiway before takeoff, c.1966.

acceptance of this suggestion was received. At 11.57 the flight reported 'by Bannow level 170 estimating Strumble at 03'. 'Change now to London Airways', the controller at Shannon instructed, adding the frequency, '131.2', and a polite 'good-day'. At 11.58, London Air Traffic Control intercepted a call (garbled and simultaneous with another call) which appeared to be 'Echo India Alpha Oscar Mike with you', and eight seconds later a call was intercepted, which was interpreted as 'Twelve thousand feet descending spinning rapidly'.

At 12.10, London Air Traffic Control advised Shannon ATC that they had no radio contact with EI-AOM. After the loss of contact, London ATC requested that Aer Lingus flight EI 362, which was heading to Bristol from Dublin, divert to an area west of Strumble to see if they could see anything on the water. They descended to 500 feet but nothing was spotted. At 12.25 a full alert was declared and by 13.36 there was a report of wreckage sighted, though searching aircraft found nothing. The following day wreckage was sighted and bodies recovered six miles north-east of Tuskar Rock. Thirteen bodies were found over the next few days and another was discovered some weeks later.

There were no survivors; all 61 on board including 4 crew perished. St. Michael's Community Centre on Green Street in Wexford was used as a temporary morgue.

Ann Kelly, a 21-year-old former Loreto student and one of the Kelly's Bakery family on Wexford's Main Street, was one of the two air hostesses on the flight. Her body was discovered in Wexford Harbour and she was the first victim to be identified. The other stewardess to perish was Mary Coughlan, also aged 21, from Tipperary town. Mary, who had qualified only a month before, was not rostered that morning on EI-AOM. She had switched flights with a colleague who needed the

The two Aer Lingus stewardesses who died. Ann Kelly (left) from Wexford and Mary Coughlan from Tipperary.

day off. Mary Coughlan's body, like those of most of the others on board, was never found.

Of the 57 passengers, there were thirty-three Irish (mostly from the Cork area), eight Swiss, six Belgian, five British, two Swedish, two American and one Dutch.

For weeks following the disappearance, searches were carried out for the wreckage by fishermen from Arklow to Ducannon. Ireland's only two seaworthy warships *LÉ Macha* and *LÉ Cliona* were deployed. British

The Memorial Park in Rosslare features a centrepiece of stone from Mount Leinster with three panels symbolizing the portholes of the aircraft in descent. (photo: Des Kiely)

vessels working on the search included *HMS Penelope, HMS Shoulton, HMS Clarbeston, HMS Iveston, HMS Nurton, HMS Bronington, HMS Reclaim* (diving and rescue) and Royal Navy salvage vessel *Uplifter*.

The main wreckage was located on the seabed two miles from Tuskar Rock. It took three months to find the fuselage and when it was first lifted out of the sea, it crashed down again into the water and sank to the bottom before finally being found again and recovered many days later. There was no black box recorder fitted to Viscounts at that time.

Of the 14 bodies recovered, the first 13 were identified and returned to their families for burial, but the 14th (a male) that was recovered weeks later was never identified and was buried in an Aer Lingus plot at Crosstown Cemetery. In 2000, the body was exhumed and a tissue sample taken. Finally in 2013 a DNA profile was established. The search is still on to find the families of 20 of the 33 males whose bodies were never recovered so that their DNA can be compared with that of the remains.

WAS THERE A COVER-UP?

Because the flight was on a clear Sunday morning, many people on the ground witnessed the plane in distress and even its final plunge into the sea. But some of these eyewitness reports were simply dismissed as inaccurate.

A report on the inquiry carried out into the accident was published in 1970. This investigation was conducted by officials of the Aeronautical Section of the Department of Transport and Power. The exact cause of the accident was not established. 'There is not enough evidence available on which to reach a conclusion of reasonable probability as to the initial cause of this accident. The probable cause of the final impact with the sea was impairment of the controllability of the aircraft in the fore and aft (pitching) plane,' it concluded.

According to Shannon Air Traffic Control records, EI-712 had travelled a meandering course over land that included two spiral dives east of Youghal and west of John F. Kennedy Arboretum – as if the pilot was trying to resolve a mechanical problem, without returning to Cork. It is believed that part of the plane's tail may have failed. Witnesses say the pilot, 35-year-old Capt. Barney O'Beirne, kept the Viscount airborne at about 1,000 feet above the water and flew on for about 15 minutes. At 11.57 it was south of Hook Head in a progressively critical condition and went into an uncontrollable spin before crashing into the sea near Tuskar Rock.

For many years the cause of the crash was rumoured to have been an RAF missile fired from a test range at Aberporth, just north of Fishguard. The British denied anything was in the air on the Sunday of the crash and Welsh launching sites were all shut.

On the 30th anniversary of the accident in 1998, there were newspaper articles and television programmes focusing on the possible involvement of UK ships and missile ranges on the Welsh coast in the downing of the aircraft. With pressure too from victims' families, it was decided that Irish and UK officials would review all files held relating to the accident to see if the cause of the accident could be established.

It was decided that 'the possibility of a cause other than a (near) collision with another airborne object being the initial cause of the upset ... does not appear to have been adequately examined in the 1970 report'. The International Study Team appointed to carry out the review published their findings in December 2001. These were the main conclusions:

Memorial overlooking Rosslare Harbour and Tuskar Rock Lighthouse, 11km off the southeast coast of Wexford. The wreckage of Flight 712 was found 3km from the lighthouse. (photos: Des Kiely)

• An initial event, which cannot be clearly identified, disturbed the air flow around the horizontal tail surfaces and the pitch control of the aircraft. In the light of what was observed by non-skilled people there was a strong indication that structural fatigue, flutter [vibration in a control surface which may cause difficulty and lead to a structural failure], corrosion or bird strike could have been involved.

• It is possible that the sensitivity of the engine fuel control units to negative accelerations imposed during the initial upset, had an adverse effect on the subsequent flight path of the aircraft.

• The severe manoeuvres of the aircraft following the initial upset and the subsequent flight would have been outside the airworthiness certification envelope and may have resulted in some deformation of the structure.

• A number of possible causes for an impairment of pitch control were examined and it is considered very possible that excessive spring tab free play resulted in the fatigue failure of a component in the tab operating mechanism thus inducing a tailplane-elevator tab free flutter condition.

• The loads induced by the flutter condition would be of sufficient magnitude and frequency to cause a fatigue failure of the port tailplane within the timescale estimated for EI-AOM.

• There was no involvement of any other aircraft or missile.

The recovery of one of the fourteen bodies taken from the sea near Tuskar Rock.

The review concluded that the original investigation in 1970 was inadequate, not least because the unit which investigated the crash was the same unit which had given the aircraft its safety clearance.

However, the review was deemed unsatisfactory by many and the Minister for Transport, Mary O'Rourke, appointed two international air accident investigators to carry out a fresh study of the original investigation: Yves Le Mercier, a retired French naval pilot and former head of the French Air Accident Investigation Branch, and Colin Torkington who was then vice-president of the International Civil Aviation Organization. Both were experienced in investigating air crashes around the world.

In their subsequent report, published in 2002, they noted that Aer Lingus paperwork relating to a routine maintenance inspection carried out on the aircraft in December 1967 was found to be missing in 1968. The report also concluded that the crash was the result of a chain of events starting with a failure to the left tailplane, which provides stability and control. Recordings

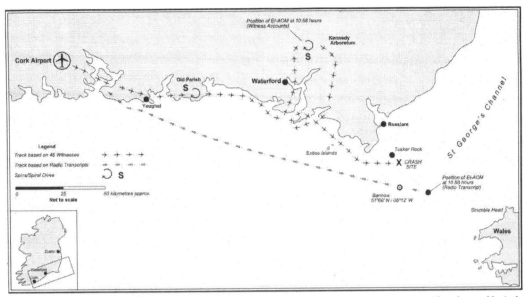

The contrasting flight paths. The 2002 report pieced together 46 eyewitness accounts to provide a clear and logical flight sequence. The upper track is verified by 46 independent witnesses. The lower track is the path, which is based on the transcripts of the radio signals exchanged between EI-AOM and the ground stations.
(From crz.com, map courtesy of M.H. Gill & Co.)

were scrubbed and this was put down to the cost of buying new tape, according to management. The report concluded that there was no missile or drone in the vicinity of the crash. There had been time for routine procedures such as switching on 'Fasten Seat Belt' signs – which were found to be lit at impact. Had the pilot experienced a sudden loss of control as with a missile strike or mid-air collision, this would have been completely implausible. The report estimated that a force of 200kg would have been required from the pilot and co-pilot on their controls to bring the plane out of its spins. The only possibility to lessen the force required would have been by throttling up, but this would have caused the plane to climb. Therefore it was impossible for the pilot to land the aircraft, as throttling back would again send the plane into a fatal dive.

Structural failure to the left tail-plane caused by metal fatigue, corrosion, flutter or a bird strike were cited as possible causes. The first spiral dive near Youghal may have been caused by the tail failing or becoming damaged, and that the second dive caused by further crippling damage.

Though the pilot was able to keep the doomed Viscount airborne, the passengers must have known that the end was near. The progressively critical condition of the aircraft finally led to an uncontrollable dive slightly to the port side that ended in impact with the sea, killing all on board.

But why would a well trained and experienced captain not have declared an emergency and radioed for assistance until a brief last message before plunging into the sea?

Analysis after the crash found that some maintenance compliance periods on the aircraft were exceeded. For example, some jobs due at 350 hours' flying time were carried out at 1,400 hours. There were two American citizens on board and Aer Lingus may also have been afraid of being sued. After three Viscount accidents in such a short space of time, Aer Lingus's reputation was now seriously damaged and maybe those RAF conspiracy theories suited them at the time.

The passengers who perished on Flight 712 included five married couples, two pairs of sisters, three children (one six months old), two shop owners, eight consultant doctors, two nurses, one priest, one orchestra conductor, one author, one holder of a CBE, one chess champion, nine businessmen, a group of Belgian business associates who were on a fishing trip and two doctors from Holland and Switzerland who were also returning from a fishing holiday in Ireland.

The 2002 report included the following statement: '...it was a major achievement for the crew to be able to keep this aircraft flying for more than half an hour, with such poor manoeuvrability characteristics. This showed a remarkable intrinsic and professional level of experience. It is equitable to acknowledge such a performance.'

The pilot, Captain Barney O'Beirne from Dublin, was an accomplished pilot with over 1,600 hours' flying experience in a Vis-

Captain Barney O'Beirne, the pilot of Flight 712.

count. At the time of his death he was one of Ireland's best-known golfers. His co-pilot, First Officer Paul Heffernan, aged 22, was from Cork. His total flying time was 1,139 hours, of which 900 was on Viscounts. In 2004, they were both posthumously awarded the Wright Brothers Award, established by the Irish Airline Pilots' Association to honour exceptional contributions to aviation in Ireland and abroad.

Bull-baiting, pike-making and killings in the Bullring

The Tholsel building and fish market with fountain outside, photographed in 1896. (photo courtesy Eddie Macken)

VARIOUSLY referred to through the years as the Common Plain, the Market Place and Fountain Square, the Bullring is situated in the very heart of Wexford town. Common Plain connected with Common Quay via Common Quay Street. Since at least 1410, when the Earl of Pembroke issued a charter to the Mayor of Wexford 'to set a fair price for goods sold in the market place', it was the location of a bustling market.

BULL-BAITING

In 1621 the Guild of Butchers declared that it would participate in the blood sport of bull-baiting twice a year on the 'Common Plain of Wexford'. The butchers were required to provide a bull twice a year, in August and November. Bull-baiting was widespread in Ireland at the time. It involved pitting a bull against a number of dogs. Bulldogs and pit bull terriers (created by breeding bulldogs and terriers together) were bred especially for the sport. The bull was collared and tied by a rope to an iron stake and the object was for the dogs to immobilize the bull. The dogs were let off one by one by their owners and, as the dog darted towards the bull to attack, the bull would attempt to catch the dog and toss it into the air. The bull eventually died from multiple dog bites. The bull's hide was presented to the Mayor and the meat distributed to the poor of the town. The 'sport' continued in the Bullring until about 1770. It was finally outlawed under the Cruelty to Animals Act of 1835.

Bull-baiting, popular in the 17th and 18th centuries, gave the Bullring its name. (illustration: Pat Nicolle)

CROMWELL

At the time of the Confederate Wars (1641-1653), the port of Wexford was being used to import arms and by 'privateers' to attack English shipping. The town was under the control of the Confederates and the command of Colonel David Synnot. When Oliver Cromwell was sent to Ireland in 1649 to put an end to the war, he had Wexford next in his sights, having first massacred about 2,000 people in Drogheda — a town that refused to surrender to his forces.

Cromwell reached Wexford on 1 October and two days later issued an order for the town to surrender. His troops captured Rosslare Fort but negotiations went on for a week between Cromwell and Colonel Synnot, who headed the Wexford garrison. The people of the town wanted Synnot to surrender and prevent a massacre. On 11 October the commander of Wexford Castle, Captain James Stafford, surrendered the castle. Cromwell's forces threw open the wall gates and poured through, killing and plundering. The town garrison, along with terrified townspeople, trapped within the town walls, gathered in the Market Place (the Bullring).

Cromwell later wrote that his troops 'put all to the sword that came in their way...' About 300 also died when two overloaded boats sank as people attempted to escape from the quays across the harbour. He claimed that in total about 2,000 'enemy', including David Synnot, perished. Six friars were killed when troops broke into the Franciscan Friary and six churches in the town were demolished on Cromwell's orders. The bells of Selskar Abbey were shipped to England and are said to be now in a church steeple in Liverpool.

Fourteen years later the Bishop of Ferns, Nicholas French, wrote in a letter that people of the town had been indiscriminately killed. Over a hundred years later, in 1758, it was claimed that 300 women and children were massacred in the Bullring by Cromwell's forces.

BUILDINGS

The Courthouse once stood at the junction of the Bullring and the Main Street. This was replaced in 1794 with the construction of the Tholsel (or 'toll house'). The Council Chamber, Corporation and Mayor's offices were located on the upper floor and on street level was the fish market, sited behind five archways. In 1795 the Marquess of Ely, Charles Tottenham of Loftus Hall, had a drinking water fountain erected outside the Tholsel, and for a time the area was known as Fountain Square. In 1808 a new Courthouse was completed on Custom House Quay, opposite Wexford Bridge. This oak bridge was the first to link the town with Ferrybank and was completed in 1795. It was to be the scene of gruesome executions and murders during the rebellion of 1798. The fountain was removed by Wexford Corporation in the 1950s for restoration and finally, some sixty years later, there are plans to re-install it in the Bullring. The current market building dates from the 1870s and the site of the Tholsel building is now occupied by Stone Solicitors.

Fishmongers in the Bullring before the Pikeman statue was installed in 1905.

THE PIKEMAN

Following on from the 'First Wexford Rebellion' of 1793 when over 90 protesters were killed by British forces in the John Street/Newtown Road area and five were hanged, an open-air munitions factory was set up in the Bullring. Blacksmiths forged pikes and repaired weapons throughout 1797 and into 1798 in preparation for the United Irishmen rebellion that finally came in the summer of that year. The rebels had most success in Wexford, having ousted the British garrison and declared a 'Wexford Republic' which lasted for three weeks.

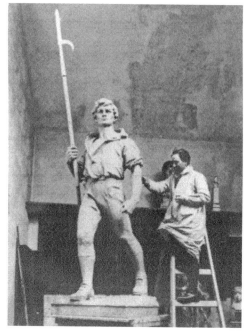

Oliver Sheppard in his studio on Pembroke Road, Dublin, in 1903 working on a clay mould for his Pikeman statue which was unveiled two years later in the Bullring. (photo: National College of Art and Design)

The centenary commemorations in 1878 were exploited by John Redmond and his Irish Parliamentary Party who linked them to the ongoing struggle for Home Rule. The Catholic Church, that had opposed the violence of the French Revolution, viewed the 1798 Rebellion as a struggle against religious oppression by the British. Father Patrick Kavanagh, a Wexford Franciscan friar and historian, was dismissive of the important role of Protestant United Irishmen leaders in the rebellion and attempted to put Catholic priests such as Father John Murphy at the centre of the insurrection. The United Irishmen, however, aimed at uniting 'Protestant, Catholic and Dissenter'.

It was agreed by the Wexford 1798 Committee to erect permanent memorials throughout the southeast but politics and division delayed the commemorations. Father Kavanagh laid the foundation stone for a Bullring monument on 1 November 1898 though there was not yet a statue made. A piece of the wooden Market Cross that once stood in the Bullring was included. Also present at the ceremony were local members of parliament: John and William Redmond, Thomas Esmonde and Peter Ffrench. The stone came from the Three Rocks on Forth Mountain, site of the famous 1798 rebel victory that resulted in the retreat of the British garrison from the town. The streets of Wexford were festooned with green bunting for the occasion as marching bands paraded into the Bullring.

Oliver Sheppard, the Dublin-born sculptor and nationalist who studied in London and Paris, was contacted by the committee. They told him: 'our idea of the monument is a figure ... of an insurgent peasant (about seven feet high) with pike in hand and in a defiant attitude'. Sheppard was sent a pike head to work with and he completed a full-scale figure the following year. This was sent to Paris where it was cast in bronze and shipped to Ireland in February 1904. The limestone pedestal was made by Carroll's of Tullamore with just the date '1798' cut into it.

The unveiling took place on 6 August 1905, again with bunting, and twenty bands paraded through the town. Special trains arrived from around the country carrying crowds to witness the spectacle. Bonfires were lit the night before and thousands crammed into the Bullring for the event. Father Kavanagh unveiled the Pikeman in the presence of the Mayor J.J. Stafford. The Pikeman is one of Sheppard's finest works and it resulted in him being commissioned to create the 1798 statue depicting Father John Murphy that stands in Market Square, Enniscorthy. In 1908 it too was unveiled by Father Kavanagh. In 1930 he also sculpted the bust of William Redmond, who was killed in action in World War I, and is located in Redmond Park.

THE MURDER OF MARYANNE WILDE

Peter Ffrench was a member of parliament for South Wexford and also a magistrate and coroner. Five years after the unveiling of the Pikeman statue he was to open an inquest on the day after the death of murder victim 18-year-old Maryanne Wilde in the Bullring.

Simon Bloom, aged 29, rented rooms above The Cape licensed premises run by Philip Keating (from 1942 operated by Con Macken). From there he ran an art and picture-framing business and on the fanlight above the entrance to his quarters was written 'S. A. Bloom'. Maryanne lived with her widowed mother on Roche's Terrace. Bloom, who was of Polish origin, employed Maryanne for just one week to take care of the business when he was in Dublin. He had been pursuing her for about a year previously. On Saturday 7 May 1910 the pair had a row after Bloom asked her to marry him. She told him she was engaged to Archie Wade, a merchant seaman from Manchester, and that they would marry in a fortnight. Bloom went into a rage, tried to choke her and then slit her throat.

An advert for Bloom's photographic business above Keating's (now Macken's) public house, from a 1900 guidebook 'In And About Wexford'.

She was later heard moaning inside the door of the hallway to Bloom's apartment by two passers-by, who alerted Bloom as they spotted him walking away towards the Main Street. Bloom returned and opened the door but ran upstairs past Maryanne and locked himself in. The two rushed Maryanne, covered in blood, on a handcart to the County Infirmary on Hill Street, where Dr. David Hadden tended to her.

When news of the attack spread, a crowd gathered outside The Cape, demanding that the police break down the door to the apartment. The owner, Mr. Keating, produced a key and when the constables entered they found Bloom had attempted to cut his own throat with a razor blade. He too was taken to the infirmary. Maryanne was still conscious and able to make a statement to the local magistrate, accusing Bloom of the attack. Maryanne died later that evening from her injuries. Bloom was subsequently tried and found guilty. After spending some years in prison he's believed to have emigrated to America.

The Church of Ireland rectory was located in the corner of the Bullring (where the Diana Donnelly boutique now stands). It is believed that the mother of Oscar Wilde, Jane Elgee, was born here in 1821. Her father Charles was the son of the Rector of St. Iberius, Rev. John Elgee.

Over the years the Bullring was the location for political rallies by such luminaries as Daniel O'Connell, Charles Stewart Parnell, John Redmond, James Larkin and Éamon de Valera. In 1998, the bicentenary of the 1798 Rebellion, the Bullring was reconstructed. A 'Tree of Liberty' was planted and a 'time capsule' was buried behind the Pikeman and President Mary McAleese performed the official opening.

Tuskar Lighthouse: horrific deaths of 15 workmen

Tuskar Rock was built on a treacherous cluster of rocks that lie southeast of Rosslare. (photo: Des Kiely)

THE AREA of sea bounded by Kilmore Quay, the Saltee Islands, Tuskar Rock and Carnsore Point is known as the 'Graveyard of a Thousand Ships'. This major intersection for shipping is full of hidden rocks and reefs that have resulted in the most shipwrecks of any location off the Irish coast. Tuskar Rock is a group of rocks 11km off the southeast coast of County Wexford and has been responsible for a recorded 176 shipwrecks. From Old Norse, the rock was named Tuskar by the Vikings, and means large (*tu*) rock (*skar*).

Ireland currently has 65 lighthouses and 53 of these were built during the 19th century, when there was something of a lighthouse building boom. In 1810, the Corporation for Improving the Port of Dublin assumed control of the country's then 14 lighthouses from the Revenue Commissioners. The board wrote to the Lord Lieutenant of Ireland, Charles Lennox, the Duke of Richmond, seeking approval for the construction of a lighthouse on Tuskar Rock. The site was surveyed by George Halpin, the prominent civil engineer and lighthouse builder, who was appointed the country's Inspector of Lighthouses that same year.

In 1867, the Commissioners of Irish Lights took control of Ireland's lighthouses and by then the number had dramatically risen from 14 to 72.

The construction of 50 of these was overseen by George Halpin.

In 1811, Halpin submitted his plans, which were similar to the Poolbeg Lighthouse at South Wall in Dublin Port. However, the Board rejected these and instead insisted that the design follow the South Stack Lighthouse near Holyhead, which had been recently completed in 1809. Waterford Chamber of Commerce wrote to the Board, giving preference to the Saltee Islands for the siting of the lighthouse but Tuskar Rock was ultimately sanctioned as the location by the Board. Building commenced in 1812 under Halpin's supervision and took three years to complete.

A tragedy occurred, however, at an early stage in construction when 25 builders, carpenters and stonemasons were stationed on the inhospitable rock in temporary cabins. On the night of Sunday 18 October 1812 a violent storm struck while the men took shelter in their precarious lodgings. In what was the worst such disaster in Ireland's history of lighthouse building, their cabins were hit by giant waves that created a vacuum, sucking 14 men into the sea. For over two terrifying days, the remaining 11 workmen clung to the slippery rocks before being finally discovered and rescued by a service vessel at 11am on the Wednesday.

As the *Wexford Herald* reported: 'When the tide fell and that part of the rock dried, the survivors proceeded to fasten a cable as tight as possible to two ring bolts about 30 yards asunder to which they bound themselves by small ropes

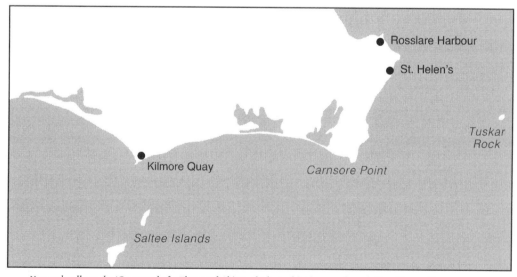

Known locally as the 'Graveyard of a Thousand Ships', the busy shipping area bounded by Kilmore Quay, the Saltee Islands, Tuskar Rock and Carnsore Point. © *Des Kiely*

around the waist; but here at the rise of the next tide they had nearly the same horror to encounter as the waves several times broke them'.

Those who drowned were named as: William Bishop, Philip Brady, Pat Byrne, Samuel Cooke, Josiah Corish, William Devereux, John Edward, John Kehoe, John Keogh, Richard Meyler, John Needham, James Nowlan, Miles Ryan and John Salmon. There were 11 survivors listed.

In another serious mishap on 22 August 1814, a stonecutter fell 22 metres (72 feet) to his death.

The lighthouse was built using silver-grey granite from the then recently opened quarry on Dalkey

Tuskar Rock, illuminated since 1815, cost the lives of 15 men during its construction.

Hill in Dublin. The stonework would eventually be concealed behind a whitewashed finish. The mirrored light, made by Robinson of London, had three faces: two white and one red. Each flashed for ten seconds at two-minute intervals. In foggy conditions a bell rang every thirty seconds. The light was first illuminated on 4 June 1815. Later in 1885, the oil lamps and reflectors were replaced with a biform lens, supplied by Edmundson of Dublin and the light was finally converted to electric in 1938.

A row of four lighthouse keepers' cottages were built in 1817 above St. Helen's Pier, which was used by relieving boats to and from the lighthouse. But by 1834, due to 'the disgraceful attitude of the keepers ashore', the keepers' families were moved out to cramped conditions in the dwelling at the base of the lighthouse. It was not until 1886 that four new lighthouse keepers' dwellings were built above Rosslare Harbour, located next to where the now derelict St. Helen's Hotel is located.

One night in 1821 at around 3am, a ship called *Shark*, en route from Le Havre to Wexford, landed at Tuskar Rock, coastguard and customs officials having been spotted patrolling close to the entrance to Wexford Harbour. The principal keeper, Michael Wisheart, and assistant keeper, Charles Hunter were asked by the skipper to 'take care' of his cargo of a large cask and several smaller kegs of French brandy, tea, candles and silks. He offered them a reward if the goods remained untouched until his return. He continued on his journey into Wexford but when he returned two days later on a small boat out of Ballytrent, he found 'Hunter dead drunk on his back, and Wisheart in the same state on his side', having broken open the cask of brandy. The skipper left them to their slumbers and took what remained of his cargo to Ballytrent.

Coincidentally, on that very same wet and windy night, King George IV was sailing towards Kingstown on board the Royal Yacht in convoy with some ships of the Royal Fleet. They failed to observe the expected light from Tuskar and so ran for shelter to Milford Haven in South Wales. An inquiry into the incident was carried out by the Corporation in the Ballast Office, Dublin. On 23 October 1821, Hunter was found guilty of aiding and abetting the smuggling of goods from France and was returned to his job as a blacksmith in the Ballast Office workshop. Michael Wisheart was demoted to assistant keeper and sent to wind-swept Skelligs Lighthouse off the County Kerry coast. Ensuring that his cow had enough grass to eat, Wisheart regularly tended his small patch. One day, while cutting the grass near the cliff's edge, he fell to his death.

The warning bell on Tuskar was replaced in 1879 by an explosive fog signal and in 1978 with an electric horn. The fog horn was sounded for the last time in January 2001.

During World War II, a drifting mine that had broken from its moorings, hit Tuskar Rock and exploded in 1941, seriously injuring two assistant keepers. They were brought ashore by the Rosslare lifeboat but one of the keepers, Patrick Scanlan, who was the grandfather of the novelist Patricia Scanlan, died in Wexford County Hospital the next day. He was a father of seven and a native of Kilrush, Co. Clare. The mine also demolished the dwellings and the Tuskar beacon was extinguished.

Tuskar Lighthouse became fully automated in 1993 when the keepers were withdrawn. Today it is controlled remotely by the Commissioners of Irish Lights in Dún Laoghaire.

The Rosslare Harbour Memorial Garden was opened in 2006 to remember the 61 passengers and crew who lost their lives in the Aer Lingus crash near Tuskar Rock in 1968. The park also contains a plaque commemorating the 14 men who perished in 1812 during the construction of Tuskar Lighthouse.

THE OTHER LIGHTHOUSES OF COUNTY WEXFORD

ROSSLARE PIER

The little lighthouse sits forlornly at the end of the pier at Rosslare Europort. The great engineer Isambard Brunel (1806-59) planned a route between Ireland and Britain via Rosslare and Fishguard. In 1882, the Fishguard and Rosslare Railways and Harbours Company constructed the pier at Greenore, later named Rosslare Harbour, and the lighthouse was commissioned in 1906. The Wexford to Rosslare Harbour railway link was built

The little Rosslare Pier Lighthouse stands at the end of the pier wall but is inaccessible, located within the ferryport security area. (photo: Des Kiely)

in the late 1800s and the route between Rosslare Harbour and Cork was officially opened in 1906. The railway used to run to the end of the pier but it is no longer possible to reach the lighthouse, as it now stands within the restricted area of the ferryport.

HOOK HEAD

The oldest intact lighthouse still in operation in the world. Its construction in the early 1200s is attributed to the Anglo-Norman knight William Marshal, who wanted to guard the entrance to Waterford Harbour. Marshal had married Isabel de Clare, the young daughter of Strongbow, and founded the medieval town of New Ross. The fortress Tower of Hook was intended to aid shipping and the monks of nearby St. Saviours of Rinn Dubháin were tasked with the job of light-keeping by night and the tower acted as a landmark by day.

Following the outbreak of civil war in 1641, the monks left the area and it was not until 1667, following the Cromwellian invasion, that the tower was re-established.

In 1704, Queen Anne transferred the lighthouses around the Irish coast to the Revenue Commissioners. However, the lease on the land on which Hook Lighthouse was built was held by the Loftus family. It was finally handed over to the Port of Dublin (the Ballast Board) in 1810. The

Hook Head Lighthouse, the world's oldest intact lighthouse still in operation. (photo: Des Kiely)

lighthouse keepers' houses were built in the 1860s and in 1933 the colours of the tower were changed from white with three red bands to white with two black bands.

The light switched to electricity in 1972 and it became fully automated in 1996, when the lighthouse keepers left the Hook after 800 years. The old keepers' houses became a visitor centre in 2001 and tours of the lighthouse are offered. The foghorn went silent in 2011 and the Hook remains a fully operational lighthouse.

DUNCANNON

There are two lighthouses that work in tandem in Duncannon – Duncannon North (the rear light) and Duncannon Fort (the front light). Together they form a pair of range lights (leading lights) that guide ships over the bar of Duncannon.

DUNCANNON NORTH: In 1817, Roche's Point Lighthouse was established to guide ships into Cork Harbour. But the original lighthouse tower was deemed too small and was replaced in 1835 by the present larger tower. The original small tower was dismantled, shipped to Duncannon and erected in 1838 as Duncannon North lighthouse. It operates as a rear leading light with Duncannon Fort. The lighthouse and three-bedroomed keeper's cottage are privately owned but the light is maintained by Irish Lights, who pay an annual rent to the owner.

Duncannon North Lighthouse

Duncannon Fort Lighthouse (photos: Des Kiely)

DUNCANNON FORT:

Dating from 1774, this is the front light of the pair of range lights at Duncannon that guide shipping up the treacherous waters of the Suir/Barrow estuary, which is full of sandbanks. By lining up this light with the Duncannon North rear light, about a mile further north, the correct approach up the river can be determined. The lighthouse is located next to the historic 16th century fortified Duncannon Fort.

CONINGBEG LIGHTSHIP

Two small rocks, known as Coningmore and Coningbeg, lie roughly south-west of Great Saltee Island. Coningmore is always above water but Coningbeg appears only at half ebb. The *Coningbeg* lightship – a floating, anchored lighthouse – was established in 1824 as an aid to shipping. It was automated in 1980 and finally withdrawn in 2007, when it was replaced by a 'superbuoy' with a 14km radius light and several smaller navigational aids.

Was stolen Tintern Abbey money used to set up the Kennedys?

Patrick Kennedy (pictured) left New Ross for America in 1849. His grandson Joseph was estimated to be between the ninth and sixteenth richest person in the United States in 1957.

LT. JOHN KENNEDY was employed as an agent at Tintern Abbey. He was accused of embezzling £80,000 (€7m in today's terms) over more than twenty years and was eventually dismissed from his position in 1818. But the money remains unaccounted for to this day. Another Kennedy, Patrick, emigrated from New Ross to Boston a generation later in 1849, the last year of the Famine. His son P. J. bought three saloons and had his own whiskey importing business while still in his twenties. P. J.'s son Joseph Kennedy became one of the wealthiest businessmen in America and his son became President of the United States. Was Tintern Abbey the source of the Kennedy fortune?

THE COLCLOUGHS

The Protestant Colclough family were in possession of the thirteenth-century Cistercian Tintern Abbey, suppressed in 1536 and granted to Anthony Colclough, an army officer who hailed from Staffordshire. They became benevolent landlords and patrons of Irish sport, culture and music and were held in high regard by their tenants. In the 18th century, they built and ran schools for them and donated land for a Catholic church in nearby Ballycullane.

John Colclough's elder brother, Caesar, inherited the Tintern estate on the death of their 49-year-old father, 'Sir' Vesey (he was never knighted) in 1794. Their mother, Catherine, was a sister of Cornelius Grogan of Johnstown Castle, who was hanged on Wexford Bridge in 1798 for the part he played in the Rebellion. Sir Vesey also had a mistress, a servant girl, and had children by her. During his stewardship of the family estate, Sir Vesey managed to lose some of the family properties.

Caesar left for London in 1789 and moved on to Paris in 1791. He was in France when his father Vesey died and he inherited Tintern but had no desire to go back to Ireland. He passed charge of the estate to his brother John while requesting that he remit £600 to him annually.

However, in 1805 John convinced Caesar to return to contest the 1806 parliamentary election. He reluctantly agreed to go home in 1805 to campaign 'contrary to my own sentiments, which have long since abandoned all the vanity and inutility of ambitious views, and many years are absorbed in the tranquil researches of useful arts and sciences.' John acted as his election manager but when Caesar returned to France in May 1806, before the election was held, he was arrested there. England had been at war with Napoleon since 1803 and of his situation in France he said it was 'the greatest misfortune that ever befell me'. While back in France and unable to leave, he was returned for County Wexford in absentia in the November election. Unable to take his seat, John was returned in his place.

THE DUEL

Another election was called by King George III the following year, 1807. This was the third since the Act of Union 1800 that created a single parliament for the United Kingdom of Great Britain and Ireland, but Catholics were still barred. Wexford had three seats representing the county: one for Wexford Borough and two for the county. The seat for Wexford Borough was taken by Richard Nevill and the county seats were filled by Abel Ram and William Alcock. But the fight for one of those county seats was an eventful one.

The hard-line conservative William Alcock of Wilton Castle in Bree was running against his friend, the popular John Colclough of Tintern Abbey. Colclough, a liberal, had been accused of 'a strong leaning to the side of the United Irishmen at the time of the Rebellion' but was declared 'perfectly cured

... of this frenzy' by the doctors at Dublin Castle in 1806. The Marquess of Ely, Charles Tottenham Loftus of Loftus Hall, another conservative, offered to buy Colclough's seat if he stood down, but he declined.

During the election campaign, William Alcock accused Colclough of attempting to poach votes from his tenants, who were obligated to vote for him. Although Colclough's defeat at the poll was imminent, Alcock requested him to respect these votes. Colclough accepted but thanked his tenants in satirical terms. Exasperated at this, he sent Colclough a challenge to a duel to defend his honour in such terms that he could not decline.

They met, along with companions, on the grounds of Ardcandrisk House, between Ferrycarrig and Killurin, on 30 May 1807, two days before the election. Both men were as courteous to each other as if offence had neither been given or taken. The two friends fired and Colclough fell back dead. Alcock went into mental shock at seeing his friend lying dead on the ground. 'That's one way of getting an election,' George Tierney, MP for Athlone later observed, sarcastically. John Colclough was waked in the family townhouse in George's Street, Wexford. His funeral procession to Tintern Abbey was said to have been one of the biggest ever seen in Wexford.

Alcock had fled after the killing but returned and was tried for murder and finally acquitted. He took the seat for County Wexford but was slowly drifting into dementia as a result of the entire episode. In Parliament he began making demands for the constituency on behalf of Waterford City, his father's old seat, for which he was not a member, and finally in 1809 was placed

"New Recipe for Ascertaining the People's Choice" – *a contemporary cartoon of the duel between William Alcock of Wilton Castle and John Colclough of Tintern Abbey in 1807.*

under medical care. With his mental health deteriorating, he entered Whitmore House asylum in London while remaining a nominal MP until 1812, and died the following year.

THIS TREE STANDS WHERE JOHN COLCLOUGH ESQ OF TINTERN ABBEY FELL IN A DUEL FOUGHT WITH WILLIAM CONGREVE ALCOCK ESQ OF WILTON CASTLE AT ARDCANDRISK ON MAY 30TH 1807

John Colclough had administered Tintern until his death in the infamous duel. The village of Tintern was located south-east of the abbey on the far side of the Ban River that flows into Bannow Bay. He established a milling enterprise close to the bridge and supplied flour to the military at Duncannon Fort (the ruin of the mill is still standing). He also developed the celebrated walled garden. He wanted to extend the lawns and gardens and his plan was to relocate the village out of sight of the abbey. As their leases expired, the tenants were moved to the new village of Saltmills and the old village of Tintern was eventually demolished.

LT. JOHN KENNEDY

The Colclough estate in the 18th century had included Ballycullane, Ballygarrett, Bannow Island, Boley, Coolroe, Curraghmore, Dunmain, Garrycullen, Kilbride Glebe, Milltown, St. Kearns, St. Leonards, Saltmills, St. Mullins, Taghmon Glebe, Tintern and Yoletown. In addition, a number of areas within Wexford town (Bride Street, The Faythe, George's Street, Hill Street, John Street and Slippery Green). John Colclough also had a house on Leeson Street in Dublin. He employed an army man, Lieutenant John Kennedy, as one of his agents. Kennedy collected rents, ran errands and kept accounts of the running of the estate. He dealt with land leases and evictions and was also employed by the Chichesters on the nearby Dunbrody estate. Following Colclough's death in 1807, Kennedy continued to act as steward of the estate. Perhaps now more aware of his own mortality, he made his will within weeks of Colclough's killing, leaving £2,000 to his own brother Henry and just £69 that he felt was due to the late John Colclough.

Still trapped in France, Caesar Colclough was unable to contest the 1812 election. The county seats were won by Frederick Flood of Ballynaslaney House and Robert Carew of Castleboro House. When Napoleon Bonaparte abdicated in 1814, Caesar was finally free to return. But by the time he came back to Tintern, approximately £80,000 had disappeared from the estate's accounts. Colclough tried unsuccessfully to pin the theft on Kennedy.

In the 1818 elections, Caesar stood along with Carew, another pro-Catholic opposition member. They were both returned after a bitter and expensive contest. In that same year, Caesar married Jane Kirwan, about twenty years his junior, but they had no children. Having married Caesar, she soon had John Kennedy dismissed. But the missing money remained unaccounted for.

When Caesar died in England in frugal circumstances in 1842, aged 76, his body was brought back for burial in the old church at Tintern. Jane went on to marry Thomas Boyse of Bannow House four years later but they soon separated and she resumed the name Colclough. In Caesar's will (his fifth), which he made on his deathbed, he left the whole of his property to Jane but this was contested by members of the Colclough family, preferring his first will. The family claimed the 1842 will had been obtained 'by undue influence and misrepresentation, as having been executed by him when not capable of exercising his judgement in such matters.' The will was finally set aside by a special jury sitting in Wexford in 1852 after a long legal battle and the estate went to Mary Colclough, Caesar's second cousin. But Jane appealed and in 1857 the case was finally settled with Jane receiving £20,000 and Mary taking possession of Tintern.

Marie Biddulph-Colclough inherited the estate in 1912. She was the last of the Colcloughs and had no family. She remained living on the property until 1959 but had the roof of the abbey removed to avoid paying rates. She offered Tintern to the State and in 1963 it was taken over by the Board of Works. Marie died in Ely Hospital in 1984.

KENNEDYS IN BOSTON

It is speculated that some of the missing fortune may have helped fund the Kennedys who emigrated from New Ross a generation later. Patrick Kennedy inherited the family farm at Dunganstown and married Maria Maiden in 1798. They had four children: John, James, Mary and Patrick. Being the eldest, John inherited the farm when their father died. Patrick was only 12 when his mother died and 17 when his father passed away. His brother James married Catherine Colfer and he too farmed the land in Dunganstown.

Patrick saw no future for himself in farming and so took a job in Cherry's Brewery at Creywell, New Ross. There, as an apprentice to his friend Patrick

Barron, he learned the skills of barrel-making. Kennedy fell in love with Barron's cousin Bridget Murphy from Cloonagh near Gusserane, and they planned to marry. Now aged 26, Patrick and Bridget decided to move to America for a better future together. He left New Ross in April 1849 for Liverpool and then on to Boston on board the *Washington Irving*. His fiancée Bridget soon followed and they married in September of that year. Patrick secured a job as a cooper in East Boston and Bridget worked in a stationery shop, which she soon bought out and expanded into a grocery and liquor store. Patrick and Bridget had five children. Their youngest, P. J. Kennedy, was born in 1858. East Boston was hit by an outbreak of cholera and tragically Patrick got infected and died, aged only 35, on 22 November 1858, the same year of P. J.'s birth.

While still in his twenties, P. J. acquired three saloons and bought a whiskey-importing business, calling it P. J. Kennedy and Company. This made him a leading figure in Boston's liquor trade. He entered politics and from 1884 to 1895 held office in the Massachusetts House of Representatives and State Senate. In 1887, he married Mary Hickey, the daughter of Co. Cork parents, and their first-born was Joseph.

Joseph lost his mother in 1923 and when his father P. J. died aged 71 in 1929, hundreds of mourners lined the streets to watch Kennedy's funeral procession and businesses in East Boston closed. His son Joseph became a millionaire businessman and politician. He married Rose Fitzgerald, daughter of John Fitzgerald, the Mayor of Boston, and they had nine children. Their second-born was John Fitzgerald Kennedy, who became President of the United States.

Their daughter Eunice married Maryland politician Sargent Shriver in 1953. Eunice Kennedy Shriver founded the Special Olympics in 1968 and the first games held outside of the United States took place in Dublin in 2003.

Patrick's son P. J. Kennedy, grandfather of JFK, was born in Boston in 1858.

Another member of the Shriver family, Josephine, married Henry Roche of Enniscorthy Castle in the early 1900s. The wealthy Roche family of Woodville House, New Ross, had bought the castle in 1898. The Roches travelled every five years back to Maryland and were due to travel in 1912 out of Cobh on the *Titanic*. But one of their children developed chickenpox and they had to cancel their plans, although their bags had already been sent ahead to Cobh.

FAMINE IN WEXFORD

The Famine of 1845-49 did not affect County Wexford as much as other parts of the country. However, the population of the county fell by about 22,000 – a twenty percent drop – through emigration.

The Graves family were shipping merchants in New Ross and the *Dunbrody* was one of eight sister ships that they commissioned in the 19th century. It was built in Quebec in 1845, the year that famine struck. The Graves' merchant vessels, designed to carry cargoes of timber, cotton and fertilizer from the Americas, were fitted out with bunks to accommodate passengers fleeing starvation in the country. The *Dunbrody* had a low rate of mortality among its passengers compared to other 'coffin ships' of the time due to

the actions of its humane captain and crew. The ship continued to be operated by the Graves until it was sold in 1869. Finally, in 1875, after 30 years' service, it ran aground on the Labrador coast, carrying a cargo of timber from Liverpool to Quebec.

A full-scale replica of the *Dunbrody* was built in New Ross dry dock and launched in 2001. The ship is permanently moored at the quayside and is a popular year-round tourist attraction.

The replica Dunbrody famine ship in New Ross. (photo: Des Kiely)

Village that was submerged by the sea after 300 years

Members of Wexford Lifeboat crew examine the ruins of the village of Rosslare Fort at low spring tide in January 2015, ninety years after the storm. (photo: Lorraine Galvin, Wexford Lifeboat)

IN A SEVERE storm in November 1924, the Rosslare sandspit was breached in two places. The small village that had grown up on the site of Rosslare Fort at Rosslare Point on the extremity of the sandspit, along with the lifeboat station, was abandoned by many. The village was connected to Rosslare by a long strip of beach. For the first time in over 300 years, Rosslare Fort now stood on an island. The winter storms and treacherous waves continued into January, when the remainder of the population escaped by lifeboat and on fishing boats. The entire village and a long stretch of sandspit were all eventually submerged.

Rosslare Fort stood in a commanding position on the southern tip of the entrance to Wexford Harbour, having been built in the late 1500s to defend the port and walled town of Wexford. Fort St. Margaret, probably a timber structure, stood on the northern side of the then narrow channel at Raven Point. The forts were reinforced by the Confederates – an uneasy alliance of Irish and Old English settlers, the result of economic, political and religious tension with England in the early 1600s.

The Confederates ruled over about two-thirds of the country, with Kilkenny as their capital, and in the Rebellion of 1641 they tried to seize control of English administration in Ireland and force concessions for Catholics. Preparations for rebellion were underway and a Catholic administration established in Wexford town. Leading Protestants were imprisoned and 79 died attempting to escape when their boat sank in the harbour. A 24-foot-deep trench was dug on the outside along the

William Petty's 1685 map, commissioned by Cromwell, shows the narrow entrance into Wexford Harbour, protected on either side by Rosslare Fort on the southern arm and Fort St. Margaret at Raven Point.

length of the town wall, the harbour was fortified and Rosslare Fort and Fort St. Margaret were strengthened. Nine cannons were placed at Rosslare Fort in preparation for an expected attack. Extra land was acquired next to the Fort and housing was built for the military.

Wexford, being the nearest harbour to Britain and the continent, became the Confederates' chief naval base. Arms and ammunition were landed on board a frigate from Dunkirk, which was dispatched by General Eoghan Roe O'Neill. Wexford and Waterford acted as bases from which English shipping was attacked. By the mid-1640s, there were forty privateering frigates laden with cannon based in Wexford. Some were crewed by Flemish and French, who cruised the seas from the Bay of Biscay to the Baltic, pillaging from English and other merchant ships. Wexford was temporarily enriched with the spoils of their piracy.

CROMWELL

Meanwhile in England, civil war had been raging between the Royalists and the Parliamentarians since 1642. King Charles I was executed and the

Parliamentarians, under Oliver Cromwell, were victorious. Cromwell vowed retribution on the Irish and to avenge their 'massacre' of Protestants. He landed at Dublin in August 1649 with 35 ships and 12,000 troops and following the slaughter of about 2,000 people in Drogheda they headed for Wexford.

Rosslare Fort was taken by a company of Cromwellian cavalrymen and foot soldiers on 2 October, attacking the Fort from the peninsula side. The Confederates, under Capt. Paul Turner, are said to have retreated to a frigate moored off the Fort but the Cromwellians turned the Fort's cannons on them and they were forced to surrender. Some historians believe that the Governor of Wexford, Capt. David Synnot and his men put up a fight before they too surrendered. The soldiers, their wives and children and other inhabitants of the area were massacred in a hollow in the sand dunes at a spot that became known as 'Cromwell's murder hole' (close to the present-day car park and main entrance to Rosslare Strand). Cromwell's support fleet was now free to enter Wexford Harbour unhindered. On landing at the Fort they unloaded their siege guns, which they moved into position on Trespan Rock ('the Rocks') in preparation for the sacking of the town. (The adjoining area is today known as Cromwellsfort).

On 3 October, Cromwell issued an order for the town of Wexford to surrender. Synnot was insisting that his garrison be allowed to leave with all their weapons and ammunition. He also sought guarantees that the Catholic clergy would come to no harm and that the privateers could sail away with their ships and stolen goods. Cromwell ran out of patience. His forces aimed their guns on the town and the garrison guarding the southern section of the town wall fled. His troops stormed the town, killing and plundering. It is estimated that 2,000 soldiers, including David Synott, were killed with only 20 of Cromwell's men perishing. About 1,500 of the townspeople and 6 Franciscan friars were massacred and many were killed in the Bullring while others drowned as they tried to flee across the River Slaney.

THE VILLAGE

Following the defeat of Wexford, the Fort became a customs post but there is little reference to the area in the 18th century. During the 1798 Rebellion, two cannon were placed on the site to repel enemy ships entering the harbour.

Rosslare Fort village c.1900. (photo courtesy Bill Kelly, Rosslare)

The village of Rosslare Fort, eventually numbering 40-50 dwellings and a school, was built mainly on sand. The houses were arranged in a square with a cobbled courtyard in the centre. In the middle of the square stood a 70-foot flagpole and just outside the square on the harbour side was the highest sand dune, known as 'Hill of 60'. From the top there was a good view of the harbour and the bay. The population numbered thirty families at its peak but this reduced to only three households according to the 1901 census. Some of its younger residents were known to throw stones at ships passing through the narrow channel and sailors would throw back lumps of coal, which would be eagerly collected and used as free fuel. Passing coal vessels kept the pilot house supplied with gratis fuel.

Revenue officers, pilots, fishermen and lifeboatmen made up the majority of the inhabitants. The harbour had two wooden jetties, one belonging to the Revenue and the second owned by the pilot. The ten resident pilots lived in the pilot house and were responsible for guiding ships into Wexford as well as bringing vessels to the Revenue jetty, where customs officers boarded. When times were busy the officers met and boarded the ships out in the bay. The first Catholic Commander of the Fort (head of customs) was a man by the name of Warren, who took charge around 1800. He was the only person with authority to fire the guns if necessary. Warren was responsible for opening the first Catholic chapel, which was located in the upstairs room of one of the houses. The Wexford shipowner, Richard Devereux, donated the Stations of the Cross, which he had purchased in Paris. The last Commander was a man named White and the customs were withdrawn in the 1850s.

In 1835, a boat belonging to the Fort coastguard was returning with supplies from Wexford and capsized. Twelve people drowned and it was believed at the time that some on board were under the influence of drink. The tragedy highlighted the risk of the location of where they were living and resulted in the opening of a lifeboat station in 1838.

An American emigrant ship, the *Pomona*, was sailing from Liverpool to New York in 1859 when it hit a sandbank in violent gales just five miles off Ballyconnigar strand near Blackwater. After two nights stuck on the bank it finally slipped off into deep water and sank. The weather had been so severe that by the time the Rosslare Fort lifeboat, towed by the steam tug *Erin*, managed to reach the *Pomona* it was too late. The ship sank with the loss of all but 24 of the 448 passengers. Of these, 316 were Irish heading for a new life in America. This tragedy resulted in a second, larger lifeboat being stationed afloat at Rosslare Fort later that year. This became known as 'Wexford No. 1' and the shore-based boat as 'Wexford No. 2'.

FETHARD LIFEBOAT TRAGEDY

The Rosslare Fort lifeboats were involved in many heroic sea rescues. A Norwegian schooner called *Mexico*, with a crew of ten, was sailing for Liverpool having left Mexico, carrying a cargo of timber in November 1913. Three months later it encountered treacherous seas and gales off the Wexford coast and was blown off course. On Friday 20 February 1914 the *Mexico* found itself

The Rosslare Fort lifeboat 'James Stevens No.15' and crew, 1914. Ned Wickham (coxswain), Jem Wickham (second coxswain), Andy Doyle, Jess Walshe, Mogue Furlong, John Mitten, John Walshe, Christy Doyle and Bill Duggan (bowman).

between the Saltee Islands and Kilmore Quay. In almost zero visibility it smashed against rocks at the Keeragh Islands, just a mile off Cullenstown strand, and began to break up.

The Fethard lifeboat (the *Helen Blake*), a 35-foot rowing boat, set off with a crew of 14. When they were a few hundred yards off Little Keeragh and attempting to row through mountainous breakers the lifeboat was lashed by three enormous waves, toppling the crew into the sea. The boat was smashed to pieces within minutes and nine of the Fethard men perished upon the rocks. The remaining five reached the island and despite their injuries managed to haul eight members of the *Mexico* crew off the doomed ship and onto the rocks. Two other members of the crew, who had earlier succeeded in launching one of the ship's boats, landed safely at Ballymadder Point.

At dawn the next day, onlookers from the coast could see that the *Mexico* was breaking up, but there was no sign of the lifeboat. The figures of a number of men could be seen on the rocks, but it was unclear who they were. The Kilmore lifeboat (*The Sisters*) attempted a rescue but was driven back by the fierce gales. Later that day, the badly mutilated bodies of the lifeboat crew began to wash up on Cullenstown Strand, against the wailings of their widows and children. For two days, attempts were made to rescue the survivors but the efforts were thwarted by the atrocious weather.

The Dunmore East lifeboat (the *Fanny Harriett*) had joined the rescue attempt as well as the Rosslare Fort lifeboat (the *James Stevens*) with a crew of fifteen, towed by the tug *Wexford*, captained by Laurence Busher, and taking over six hours to reach the Keeraghs. But the continuing fierce gales forced them to shelter at Cheekpoint and later Waterford Harbour. The bad weather continued all through the next day and no rescue could be attempted. One of the *Mexico* crew died on the island from hypothermia. Early on Monday morning, two of the survivors were finally rescued by the Dunmore East lifeboat, having been perilously hauled from the island through huge waves using a lifebuoy.

The Rosslare Fort Lifeboat memorial in the Burrow, Rosslare. A wreath is laid annually to commemorate the rescue of the Norwegian schooner 'Mexico' in 1914. (photo: Des Kiely)

The Rosslare Fort lifeboat arrived after a 5-hour trip from Waterford Harbour, with Ned Wickham at the helm. The lifeboat had a 13-foot dinghy in tow and Ned sent his brother Jem, who was second cox, and bowman Bill Duggan (also a resident of the Fort) on the dinghy to rescue the rest of the survivors, two at a time. The dinghy was pierced by a rock but Jem stuffed the hole with a loaf of bread wrapped in an oilskin, which they had brought with them in case they too got stranded on the island. At great risk, they ferried the remaining ten men, two at a time, from the ice-cold rocks to the lifeboat.

The story of the tragedy and rescue was reported across the world. In appreciation, King Haakon of Norway and the Norwegian Government made substantial contributions to the benefit of the bereaved families of the Fethard lifeboatmen. Private donations were also sent to Fethard with some ending up in Fethard, County Tipperary, and so this led to the official name change to Fethard-on-Sea to avoid any further confusion.

YOLA

Due to its isolated location, the distinct Yola dialect and culture are believed to have survived in the Fort village into the mid-1880s. Yola (itself meaning *old*) was commonly spoken in the south-east baronies of Forth and Bargy. It came with the Norman Invasion of 1169 and is thought to have evolved from Middle English, which had in turn replaced Old English as the spoken language following the Norman Conquest of England. However, the Famine and emigration led to Yola gradually dying out in the 1800s. Here are the first lines of a Yola poem, as originally written down:

EE MÝDHE OV ROSSLAARÈ

'Cham góeen to tell thee óa taale at is drúe
Aar is ing Rosslaarè óa mýdhe geoudè an drú
Shoo wearth ing her haté óa ribbonè at is blúe
An shoo goeth to ee faaythè earchee deie too…

THE MAIDEN OF ROSSLARE

I'm going to tell you a tale that is true
There is in Rosslare a maid good and true
She wears in her hat a ribbon that is blue
And she goes to the faythe every day too…

SILTING, EROSION AND DECLINE

In the mid-1800s, the outline of Wexford Harbour changed dramatically with the formation of the North and South Slobs. The Redmond family were behind the reclamation project that resulted in lessening the flow of water into the harbour, causing serious silting from the River Slaney.

The aftermath of the storm that eventually washed away the village in the winter of 1924-25. (photo courtesy Bill Kelly, Rosslare)

The declining population resulted in more than half of the houses of the Fort village being deserted by the 1870s, though the village attracted many summer visitors and some of the empty houses were used as summer accommodation.

Wexford Harbour suffered a huge decline and sailing ships were being replaced by larger steamships that sought an alternative harbour. A site close to Ballygeary was chosen and named Rosslare Harbour. In 1882 the Wexford to Rosslare Harbour railway line opened with plans underway to build new ports with facilities at Fishguard and Rosslare Harbour, and develop a new steamship link. The new route began operations in 1906 with the completion of works and the opening of Rosslare Harbour train station.

The last schoolteacher, Miss Shanahan, left Rosslare Fort in 1882 to open a private school on Wexford's North Main Street on a site now occupied by the Ulster Bank. Shortly after the founding of the Irish Free State in 1922, the first free 'school bus' service, paid for by the Department of Education, was established between the Fort and Rosslare. The twice-daily service was run by Robb Duggan of Rosslare, who took the few children of the village by horse-drawn vehicle on the three-mile journey along the beach to Rosslare, but the service was tide dependent.

END OF AN ERA

Late in 1924 during a fierce gale, what people believe was a tidal wave hit Rosslare sandspit, breaching it in two places and cutting the village off from Rosslare. Huge damage was caused to the houses in the village, forcing many to flee. Damage had already been done back in 1914 in the storm that wrecked the *Mexico*, but these storms continued throughout the winter and by the middle of January most of the buildings, including the lifeboat station, were engulfed by the sea. Now an island, the wind-swept settlement was completely abandoned and eventually reclaimed by the sea.

The lifeboat coxswain, Ned Wickham, was succeeded by his brother Jem and the lifeboat was kept at Wexford quay until 1927, when the present station was opened at Rosslare Harbour. Jem continued as coxswain until he retired in 1941 and Ned later opened a restaurant on Wexford's North Main Street. Their father Thomas had been awarded a Silver Medal by the RNLI in 1896 for his long and gallant services as coxswain. For their bravery in the *Mexico* rescue, Ned was awarded a Silver Second-Service Clasp and Jem as well as Bill Duggan were awarded Silver Medals by the RNLI. Ned was again awarded a Silver Second-Service Clasp for the rescue of five men from the schooner *Mountblairy* in 1929. Ned Wickham was decorated by five countries for work rescuing life at sea – Ireland, Britain, Norway, Denmark and the Netherlands. He and Bill Duggan were also awarded Gold Medals by the GAA – the only two people in Ireland to win the award outside the field of sport.

Jem built six houses for family members overlooking Rosslare Harbour and they are still standing today. He gave them galvanized roofs and sides and from this the development got the name 'Tintown'. The flagpole that once stood in the middle of the village square at the Fort was moved to a spot in front of the houses and can still be seen there today. At low tide and after storms, what remains of the buildings – a few pieces of barnacle-encrusted masonry – occasionally appear on the surface and are sometimes visible from Raven Point.

Artist's impression of how Rosslare Fort village looked based on historical records. (courtesy artist Brian Cleare)

How *The Guinness Book of Records* began in Castlebridge

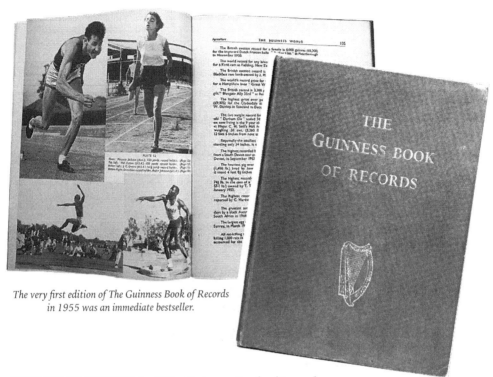

The very first edition of The Guinness Book of Records in 1955 was an immediate bestseller.

THE FIRST EDITION of *The Guinness Book of Records* (as it was called then) was published on 27 August 1955. It had a lime-green cover and stretched to a slim 198 pages. The idea to publish came four years earlier when the managing director of Guinness Breweries was on a visit to Castlebridge House, the home of Joshua Nunn.

The malting industry in Castlebridge began with the arrival of Nicholas Dixon in 1742. He bought land in the village and ran a large farm. He also set up a milling and malting business, was the owner of the main public house in the village and became the biggest local employer. The passing of Foster's Corn Law in 1784 meant that grain exports from ports other than Dublin were subsidized and this led to increased tillage in the Castlebridge area.

The first bridge across the Slaney, linking Ferrybank with Wexford town, was opened in 1795 and a toll was levied on goods being transported across it. This provided an incentive to develop boat transport between Castlebridge and the Slaney, giving direct access on to Wexford town and thus avoiding the toll. Dixon undertook to construct a canal, a number of docks and bridges in the early 1800s. Grain and malt were transported by cot, a flat-bottomed sailing boat, directly to Wexford Quay, from where they were shipped to Dublin and beyond. A cot carried 15 tons which, if transported by road, would have required some 30 horses and carts. The canal was dug out by hand and replaced the original river through the village. Dixon had Castlebridge House built in 1814.

Nicholas Dixon's son Thomas was the notorious 1798 Rebellion leader who, along with his wife Margaret Roche, was responsible for leading the massacre of nine-seven Loyalists on Wexford Bridge on the last day of the insurrection. His other son, Father James Dixon, a curate in Crossabeg, was deported to Australia the following year, charged with membership of the United Irishmen. He became the first Catholic priest to be permitted to say Mass in the new territory in 1803.

The barley-malting business passed down to Dixon's other son John, until it became insolvent in 1826 and was purchased by Patrick Breen. The Breen family moved into Castlebridge House and had the building reconstructed. In 1858, Breen commissioned the fine cast-iron conservatory from James Pierce of the Mill Road Iron Works (later Pierce's Foundry).

In 1870, Breen's granddaughter Barbara married William Bolton Nunn, who took over the running of the business in 1874 and began trading as W. B. Nunn & Co. This was the beginning of a 100-year connection between

Castlebridge House and the historic conservatory built by Pierce's Foundry in 1858.

the Nunns and Guinness Brewery in Dublin. They supplied malted barley to the St. James's Street Brewery, transporting directly from Castlebridge to Wexford Quay and on their own ships to Dublin. W. B. Nunn also had extensive business interests in China, Argentina, Brazil, Mexico, Australia and South Africa. They also had malting houses on King Street and Mulgannon Road in Wexford town (the new garda station now stands on the site).

Joshua Loftus Nunn, a nephew of William, acquired the business in 1910 and William died in 1918. Castlebridge House then came into the ownership of Joshua, who was born at Alma House, Park, Wexford in 1889. He practised as a solicitor in George's Street.

Close to Castlebridge is the North Slob, an area of 1,000 hectares of mudflats that was reclaimed in the mid-1800s by building a sea wall and creating new agricultural land. The North Slob began to attract wildfowl and then shooting parties before being made a nature reserve. Wexford Wildfowl Reserve, occupying about 200 hectares, opened in 1974.

On 10 November 1951, Sir Hugh Beaver of Guinness Breweries was on such a shooting trip to the North Slob in the company of Joshua Nunn and other associates. Beaver was an English-South African engineer and industrialist who had been director general of Britain's Ministry of Works during WWII. Knighted in 1943, he was appointed managing director of Guinness, then the largest brewery in the world, in 1946.

Sir Hugh Beaver was unable to down any golden plovers on the trip and suggested that the bird must be the fastest game bird in Europe. This started an argument over which was the fastest, the golden plover or the grouse.

Beaver was correct: it is the golden plover. But that evening in the sitting room of Castlebridge House, neither he, Joshua Nunn nor their friends were able to find a reference book that provided the answer.

Beaver knew that there must be similar questions debated nightly in the over

Joshua Nunn (left) and Sir Hugh Beaver, managing director of Guinness Breweries, who went on a shooting party on that fateful day in 1951.

81,000 pubs in Britain and Ireland, but there was no book in the world with which to settle arguments about records. He realized that a book supplying the answers to pub-goers could prove popular. Again, Beaver was correct. Figuring it might be a great marketing ploy for Guinness, he eventually decided to create one.

He later recalled that incident on the North Slob with Guinness employee Christopher Chataway, a long-distance runner. Chataway recommended his old university friends Norris and Ross McWhirter to take up the challenge of publishing a book of records. The twin brothers, both of whom had encyclopedic memories, were sports journalists and ran a fact-finding agency in London 'to supply facts and figures to newspapers, yearbooks, encyclopedias and advertisers.' After a successful interview in 1954, in which the Guinness directors enjoyed testing the twins' knowledge of records and unusual facts, the brothers were commissioned to compile the first edition of *The Guinness Book of Records*. A thousand copies were printed and given away free as conversation pieces to patrons enjoying a pint of the black stuff. 'It was a marketing giveaway, it wasn't supposed to be a moneymaker', Sir Hugh Beaver later explained.

So successful was the book that Guinness World Records Limited was established in London's Fleet Street. The first slim hardback volume was published in August 1955 and by Christmas was Britain's top-selling book. After four reprints, 187,000 copies sold in the first year. The book, called *Guinness World Records* since 1999, is published in 100 countries and 37 languages and is the bestselling copyrighted book of all time, itself a world record.

In 1974 and 1975, the Provisional IRA carried out a 14-month campaign of gun and bomb attacks in London, killing 35 people. Ross McWhirter was an outspoken critic of the IRA and advocated various restrictions on the freedom of the Irish community in Britain. He suggested that it should be compulsory for all Irish people to register with the local police and provide signed photographs of themselves when booking into hotels and hostels or renting flats. McWhirter also offered a £50,000 reward for information leading to a conviction for several recent high-profile bombings in England that were publicly claimed by the Provisional IRA. He described this himself as 'a bounty.'

On 27 November 1975, Ross McWhirter was shot and killed outside his London home by two IRA volunteers, Harry Duggan and Hugh Doherty. They were later involved in a police chase through London streets on 6 December 1975 when, along with two other IRA men, they took a middle-aged married couple hostage in the front room of their flat in Balcombe

Norris McWhirter (left) with his twin brother and Guinness Book of Records co-founder Ross in 1974. A year later, Ross was murdered by the IRA.

Street. The men demanded a plane to fly all six of them to Ireland but this was refused by Scotland Yard and so began a six-day stand-off between the men and the police. The four IRA members finally surrendered in what became known as the 'Balcombe Street Siege'.

Norris McWhirter, the surviving brother, continued to edit the *Guinness Book of Records* until 1985. He was unsuccessful in a defamation case that he took against ITV in 1985 for the programme *Spitting Image,* which had imposed McWhirter's face on the body of a naked woman. He presented the BBC television show *Record Breakers* until 1994 and died aged 78 in 2004.

W. B. Nunn & Co. was bought out by Guinness in 1973 and on the death of Joshua Nunn in 1974, Castlebridge House and surrounding lands were purchased by Wexford County Council. The last member of the Nunn family to be born in Wexford was Major Anthony Nunn, who died in England in 2013.

Castlebridge House was used at one stage as a fire-service training centre. The building has since fallen into disrepair and the historic conservatory, an irreplaceable piece of Wexford's industrial heritage, has been covered by a galvanized shed to protect it from further decay. It is hoped that the house may become a tourist attraction, with interest expressed by Diageo, the current owners of Guinness, and the Pattison Group, who own the rights to *Guinness World Records.*

Wexford town in 1764: 'fine women, beer and oysters'

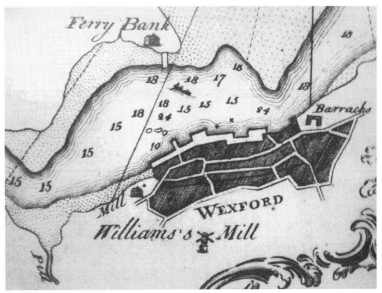

Detail from a 1764 chart of Wexford harbour and town by Dublin land surveyors Bernard Scalé and William Richards.

BY THE second half of the 1700s, Wexford town had adapted to the new enforced social and religious structures introduced in the previous century. Following the Cromwellian campaign in 1649-53 and the Williamite war in 1689-91, social, economic and political life was now in the hands of the British and Protestant elite.

After two centuries of discrimination, inequality and land confiscation, there was enormous Catholic resentment. Religious prejudice dominated Irish life. The Penal Laws were in force until the late 1700s. These excluded the majority Catholic population from voting and from holding public office. Catholic priests were prohibited from preaching and there was a bounty for arresting a priest. New Catholic churches were to be built from wood, not stone, and away from main roads. Another law stated that 'No person of the popish religion shall publicly or in private houses teach school, or instruct youth in learning within this realm'. Converting from Protestantism to Roman Catholicism was outlawed and there was a ban on Catholics having custody of orphans. Intermarriage with Protestants was banned, Catholics were excluded from the legal professions and the judiciary and there was a ban on foreign education. Catholics were also excluded from keeping firearms and prohibited from owning a horse valued at over £5 (in order to keep horses suitable for military activity out of Catholic hands).

Discontent within the Catholic population was on the rise. The Catholic Committee was founded in 1757 and before long every county in Ireland had a committee, usually headed by Catholic merchants. *The Freeman's Journal,* a nationalist newspaper, was established in 1763. They would later report on international events such as the American Revolution in 1776 and the French Revolution in 1789. These stirred up revolutionary and republican feelings in the Catholic population, leading to the setting up of the Society of the United Irishmen in 1791.

But Wexford town was now enjoying commercial prosperity and the Protestant establishment were building new houses for themselves in the George's Street, Selskar Street and Main Street areas. They were improving the streets and the town was becoming a fashionable destination. Wexford town had over 200 small malting houses and the busy port was shipping malt on 100 vessels to the Dublin distilleries and beyond to mainland Europe.

St. Iberius Church on North Main Street, c.1900. It was being remodelled for its centenary in 1770 when Amyas Griffith visited in 1764. (National Library of Ireland)

Published between 1762 and 1764 and printed in Dame Street, Dublin, the *Dublin Magazine* was a short-lived publication. It comprised miscellaneous articles of Irish interest as well as features taken from English publications with accompanying line drawings. It also listed births, marriages and deaths in Ireland.

Amyas Griffith, born in Roscrea, Co. Tipperary in 1746,

was a prolific writer of letters, poetry and plays in the second half of the eighteenth century. He was a former Inspector General of Excise for Munster and from 1780 to 1785 was Surveyor of Belfast. St. Iberius Church was being remodelled for its centenary year in 1770 at the time and the first wooden Wexford Bridge was not yet built when Griffith submitted the following article to the *Dublin Magazine* in 1764:

AMYAS GRIFFITH *Esq.*

Engraving attributed to John Wilson, printer and publisher. (National Library of Ireland)

"It [Wexford town] before Cromwell's time was well enclosed, part of the walls are yet standing, with four gates, one at each quarter of the town. The Main Street from the West-gate to the Barrack-gate is about three-quarters of a mile in length. Outside of the West-gate is a fine Spa, reckoned by skilful physicians an infallible cure for many disorders … among others the scurvy, gout, and decay. It creates an appetite and certainly dispels melancholy, &c. Beyond the South [or Barrack] gate stands the barrack, a large, low building forming a little square. I have heard it can contain 4 Companies completely. From this barrack runs a very broad street upwards of a mile in length named the Fierth, commonly styled Faith. The cabbins, which compose this suburb or outlet are very snug and commodious, and the dwellings are a set of the most industrious people on the earth. Their employments are mostly weaving nets or spinning hemp.

To return to the town. In the midst or heart of the Main Street is the bull-ring, where the Court-House, with an excellent clock, &c., stands…. About 50 yards from the Court-house, southwards, is the new Church, which, (when finished), in miniature will come nigh in beautiful structure, workmanship, materials, &c., to any in Dublin. Between the Church and Barracks, a little above the Jews Bridge, lies the gaol, it is but ordinary, yet built exceeding strong, with a court-yard, &c. In John-street, north-west of the town, is the Chapel; it is one of the prettiest I have ever seen, with a friary, garden, &c., belonging to it. The Chapel yard is esteemed the best walk about the town. We have a prodigious number of other streets, lanes and quays, as the Flesh Market, Corn Market, Back Street, Shambles, Keizars lane, Ferry-boat quay, Medow's quay, Bennett's quay, the Common quay, Gibson's lane, the Custom house quay, which is the chief or principal of all the other quays, half of which I have not mentioned. The Custom-house quay is small, but vastly pretty, with seats all round, a good warm watch-house, and an excellent Custom-house, with convenient stores, &c.

I procured the number of houses in the town and suburbs from the Collector of the Hearth money who told me there were exactly to a house, 1300, and in the confines of the walls 650 good slated houses.

For ale and oysters Wexford is noted as having the best on earth. The chief exports are Corn, which annually exceeds upwards of 2,000,000 barrels [possibly exaggerated], herrings, beer, beef, hides, tallow, butter, &c., and they trade to all parts of the globe, but in particular to Liverpool, Barbados, Dublin, Norway, and Bordeaux. Wexford imports brandy, rums, sugars, wines, dyestuffs, porter, fruit of all foreign kinds, salt, timber and hops.

Wexford is as celebrated for its fine women as for its beer and oysters'.

— *Amyas Griffith*

A view of Wexford town in 1820, from a painting by Captain H. Mitchell, dedicated to Prince Frederick, Duke of York, son of King George III. The Duke was Commander-in-Chief of the British army at the time of the 1798 Rebellion. (National Library of Ireland)

Ireland's largest brackish (fresh/saltwater) lagoons

Lady's Island Lake in the foreground with Tacumshin Lake in the distance, photographed in 1965. Tacumshin Lake was then open to the sea. (photo © Cambridge University)

LYING in the south-east corner of the county are the natural brackish lagoons of Lady's Island Lake and Tacumshin Lake, just over one kilometre apart. Brackish has a mix of fresh water and salt water, but not as much as seawater. Both lagoons are separated from the sea by a barrier of sand, gravel and small dunes with no natural outlets, and are areas of great ecological significance.

Lady's Island Lake, formerly Lough Togher (*'Lake of the Causeway'*), covers an area of 466 hectares and is one of the largest and possibly the best example of a true lagoon in the whole of Europe. It is the only surviving major example of a back-barrier seepage lagoon in Ireland. Fresh water enters from surrounding streams and percolates through the sand barrier. In winter the water level rises, flooding bordering farmland. Seawater seeps through the sandbar and also washes over it in stormy conditions. To relieve flooding, a cut through the sand barrier is made with diggers in springtime, usually in March or April, when the water levels are highest. The water then flows out into the sea for several days until the lagoon level falls below the high-tide mark.

The lagoon then becomes tidal, bringing seawater into the lagoon until the breach eventually seals up again naturally with beach sediment, gradually building up and finally stabilizing. The saltwater element of the lagoon reaches over 30% in summer.

Lady's Island Lake is an important breeding ground for terns. It is home to over 1,200 pairs of Sandwich terns and has the second-largest colony in Europe of the rare roseate tern.

In 1941, a German warplane made an emergency landing on the sand barrier separating the lake from the sea, known as Rostoonstown Strand. (See separate story *'When Hitler's Luftwaffe Bombed County Wexford'*).

Tacumshin Lake is also a shallow natural lagoon and is the larger of the two, covering 559 hectares. Older maps show that the western end of the mainly gravel barrier was once open to the sea. In the early 1970s the lagoon became separated from the sea when the sandspit extended across its mouth. A cut through the sandbar is made here too at the end of winter to lower the lagoon's water level, resulting in large areas drying out in summer.

Both Lady's Island Lake and Tacumshin Lake are the best-documented lagoons in Ireland, with regular scientific investigations carried out on their fauna and flora. They are popular with bird watchers and Tacumshin holds internationally important numbers of Bewick's swans, brent geese, wigeons, oystercatchers, golden plovers and lapwings.

The annual cut through Lady's Island Lake sand barrier releases water into the sea, lowering the level in the lagoon. However, plans are underway for the construction of an automated tunnel. (photo: Graham Murphy)

Remains of the 13th century De Lamporte castle at Lady's Island. In the distance is the parish Church of the Assumption, built in 1864. (photo: National Library of Ireland, early 1900s)

DE LAMPORTE CASTLE

Lady's Island was granted to the De Lamporte (later Lambert) family at the time of the Anglo-Norman invasion of Ireland in the late 12th century. Rudolph, son of Milo de Lamporte, built a castle here in 1237. A later member of the family was William de Lamporte, born in Wexford town in about 1611. William was burnt at the stake by the Spanish Inquisition in 1659. He was known in Mexico as 'Guillén Lombardo' and in Hollywood as *Zorro*. All that remains of the castle today are the granite tower house and gatehouse. The small tower, which was built on unstable ground and is leaning at about 30 degrees, was part of a fortified wall enclosure around the castle. Lady's Island is a causeway but is believed to have once been an island and the castle was accessed from the mainland by a drawbridge.

The tower house also protected a site on the causeway occupied by Augustinian friars from the mid-15th century. The castle was plundered and burnt by Cromwellian soldiers in 1649 and when the friars refused to join the ranks of Cromwell and march to the siege of Wexford they were killed.

PLACE OF PILGRIMAGE

An older name for Lady's Island was Cluain na mBan (*'Meadow of the Women'*), said to be named after female druids who may have worshipped there in pre-

Christian times. The locality is considered to have been a centre of druidical worship and was used during the August festival of *Lughnasa*.

In Christian times it was re-dedicated to the Virgin Mary and has been a centre of pilgrimage since the 13th century. It is the oldest Marian shrine in Ireland and second only in importance to Knock shrine in Co. Mayo. An annual pilgrimage takes place between 15 August (the Feast of the Assumption of Mary) and 8 September (the Nativity of Mary) with pilgrims numbering over 50,000 travelling from near and far. They walk around the island reciting the rosary and Masses are said twice daily.

The parish of Our Lady's Island includes Broadway, Carne, Carnsore, Churchtown, St. Helen's, St. Margaret's and Tacumshane. The parish church, the Church of the Assumption, was designed by Edward Pugin, the son of the famous Victorian architect Augustus Pugin. The church contains a relic – a crucifix that was found at the bottom of the lake in 1887 by a boy named Cogley. The tradition is that it had been seized from the now-ruined church on the island in 1649 by a man named Duffy as Cromwell's troops approached. Duffy was shot down as he tried to flee across a shallow part of the lake and the crucifix was lost for over 200 years.

The Tacumshane windmill photographed in 1935.
(photo: Albert Eskeröd/Dúchas)

TACUMSHANE WINDMILL

The beautifully preserved and maintained windmill can be found in the nearby village of Tacumshane. It was built in 1846 by Nicolas Moran as a flour mill. By 1891 there were 13 windmills operating along the south Wexford coast pumping water from the land, due to extensive land reclamation in the 19th century. The Tacumshane windmill eventually fell into disrepair however and in 1930 was acquired by Garry Murphy who replaced parts of the machinery and it functioned again until 1936, making it the oldest commercially operated windmill in the country. In 1948 it came under the care of the Board of Works who carried out repairs to it and in 1952 it was designated a national monument. The windmill is located at the rear of Meyler's Millhouse Bar & Restaurant, where the key can be obtained.

CARNSORE POINT

Nearby Carnsore Point, where the south coast meets the east coast of Ireland, was the proposed location for the country's first nuclear power plant in the 1970s. Following a series of protests and concerts organized by anti-nuclear groups at Carnsore between 1978 and 1981, the government climbed down. The protests were a massive success and in 2003 the ESB instead opened a wind farm with 14 wind turbines on the site.

SIGGINSTOWN CASTLE

Sited near Tacumshin Lake, this four-storey tower house was built by the Siggins family in the early 1500s. A brick house was added, possibly in the late 1600s. After Cromwell, it was granted to William Jacob, one of his army lieutenants, in 1667. The ruins were bought in 2016 by an American couple, Gordon and Liz Jones, who have taken on restoring the castle and attached house and adding on a 21st century living area. They sponsored a student design competition for the renovation which will take a number of years to complete.

16th century Sigginstown Castle under renovation in 2019. (photo: Des Kiely)

Battle-scarred Duncannon Fort witnessed many bloody wars

The fortified Duncannon Fort with ramparts to defend the inner buildings. (photo: Des Kiely)

DUNCANNON FORT was constructed between 1587 and 1590 in the reign of Queen Elizabeth I on the site of Duncannon Castle, which was occupied by the Etchinghams, who also had the castle at Ballyhack and a house at Dunbrody Abbey. Duncannon (in Irish 'Dún Canann' or *Conan's Fort*) may have been named after the 3rd century Celtic warrior Conan. The fort, 15km north of Hook Lighthouse, controlled the strategic shipping lane through Waterford Harbour. The three sister rivers of the Barrow, Nore and Suir flow into the estuary that gives access to Waterford, New Ross and beyond.

The fort was built following rumours of a possible attack by the Spanish, using Catholic Ireland as a back door to invade Protestant England. The fort is star-shaped and built on a strategic rocky promontory on the County Wexford side of Waterford Harbour. The fort at Passage East on the opposite side commanded the western flank. Duncannon Fort was fortified to withstand attack by cannon and dominates the village of Duncannon. It was surrounded by a 30-foot-deep dry moat with a drawbridge, gate and gatehouse, and its major buildings enclosed a central parade ground. Guns faced upriver and downriver along the sides and cannons were aimed across the estuary.

CONFEDERATE WARS

Charles I succeeded to the throne of England, Scotland and Ireland in 1625. Over the previous one hundred years, following the Tudor conquest of Ireland, lands in Munster and Ulster had been confiscated and handed to English and Scottish settlers. This led to the Confederate Wars in Ireland (1641-1653) between the Catholic gentry and clergy on one side and the Protestant and Scottish Presbyterian planters on the other. After the Rebellion of 1641 that began in Ulster, the Irish Catholic Confederation was set up, with Kilkenny as its capital.

In 1642 about 1,000 Confederate rebels were unsuccessful in taking the strategic Duncannon Fort. When 150 English soldiers arrived at nearby Redmond Hall (now Loftus Hall), which they considered sympathetic to the Confederates and was then occupied by Alexander Redmond, they were wiped out by Confederates in a surprise ambush. At Ramsgrange Castle, twenty-three Confederates were captured and eighteen of them hanged. The castle and village were burnt to the ground. In response, eighteen English soldiers, who had attacked Dungulph near Fethard, were hanged.

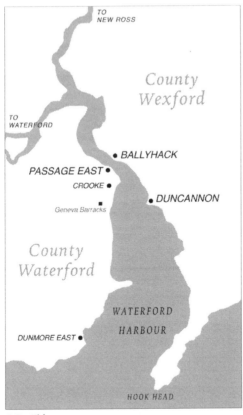

© Des Kiely

In 1645, the Irish Confederate Leinster Army, with 1,300 men under General Thomas Preston, successfully laid siege to the Fort, whose English garrison was under the command of Laurence Esmonde. Now in his mid-70s, Esmonde was the son of Walter Esmonde of

Johnstown Castle and his wife Margaret, originally from Horetown. He had been governor of Duncannon Fort since 1606.

In the two-month Siege of Duncannon, the Confederates surrounded the stronghold on its landward side. From the high ground overlooking the fort, they managed to sink one of four English supply ships, their flagship the *Great Lewis*, drowning 200 on-board soldiers. This was a huge morale boost for the Confederate rebels. The garrison finally surrendered, having run out of gunpowder and fresh water, which they sourced from a well outside the walls. The taking of Duncannon Fort was important for the Confederates as it meant that the sea route into Waterford was now free of hostile English shipping. (The wreck of the *Great Lewis* was discovered off Duncannon in 1999 and this is now a protected site.)

CROMWELL

King Charles I was accused of complicity in the rebellion in Ireland. He was executed by the Parliamentarians in 1649. Oliver Cromwell was chosen to command the forces that would bring an end to the Confederate Wars in Ireland and punish the Irish for their mistreatment of Protestants. The Confederates were in control of Wexford town and the port was used for the importation of arms. Following the brutal Siege of Wexford in October 1649 and the surrender of New Ross, Cromwell was set on attacking Waterford, a city that had expelled its Protestant inhabitants, transporting them to England in 1642.

Oliver Cromwell, 'Lord Protector of the Commonwealth of England, Scotland and Ireland' from 1653 to 1658.
(National Library of Wales)

Henry Ireton, the English Parliamentary commander and son-in-law of Cromwell, unsuccessfully attacked Duncannon Fort but succeeded in capturing the fort at Passage East, enabling him to bring siege guns up by sea. The first attack on Waterford late in 1649 failed. But on 10 August 1650, after a nine-month siege of the city, its garrison under General Thomas Preston surrendered to Ireton. The city had run short of food and 400 people a week within the city walls were dying of plague. Duncannon Fort, after a lengthy

The flight of King James II from Duncannon Fort to France following his defeat by William of Orange at the Battle of the Boyne on 12 July 1690. (Artist: Romeyn de Hooghe, National Library of Ireland)

blockade, also surrendered on 12 August, thus bringing an end to over a decade of hostilities on the Hook Peninsula. Kilkenny, the Confederate capital, surrendered in May 1650 and when Cromwell left Ireland two months later, most of the country was in English hands.

FLIGHT OF JAMES II FROM DUNCANNON FORT

James II, son of the executed Charles I, succeeded as King of England, Scotland and Ireland in 1685. He was Catholic and unpopular with the Protestant majority in Britain. James's 15-year-old daughter Mary had married the Protestant Dutch Prince William of Orange and in 1688, William and Mary deposed James as king in what became known as the 'Glorious Revolution' and James fled to France.

Ireland remained loyal to James and attempted, with the help of French forces, to overthrow William. But the Jacobites were defeated by the Williamites in the Siege of Derry and the Battle of the Boyne in 1690. The Battle of Aughrim in Co. Galway in 1691 was the final decisive battle won by the Williamites and was the bloodiest ever fought on Irish soil, resulting in about 7,000 deaths.

Following his defeat at the Battle of the Boyne, James travelled with a small escort from Dublin to Duncannon Fort and set sail for Kinsale. From there he returned to exile in France, never to return to Ireland. After his speedy exit from the battlefield, his supporters gave him the nickname 'Séamus an Chaca' (*James the Shit*). Following its surrender to his troops without resistance, William stayed at the fort, from where he departed for England.

The pier at Duncannon was constructed in the eighteenth century and the Fort Lighthouse, built in 1774, remains in use today.

1798 REBELLION

During the Rebellion of 1798, the fort did not fall into the hands of the United Irishmen and remained under British control. Following the outbreak of the Wexford Rebellion, a contingent of the Meath Militia, numbering about ninety, were marching from Duncannon Fort to Wexford town to reinforce the garrison there. The troops were all but wiped out in an ambush at Three Rocks, at the foot of Forth Mountain, by a rebel army of about 10,000 that had camped on the mountain overnight in preparation for an assault on Wexford town the next day. In the fifteen-minute battle that ensued, the rebels took three cannons, arms and ammunition. When the insurgents entered the town, their number totalled about 20,000 and the remaining English garrison of 1,200 retreated. Duncannon Fort became a place of sanctuary for fleeing loyalists and soldiers during the rebellion.

Many captured rebels were imprisoned and some executed at the fort. Others were held, and many tortured, on the opposite side of the estuary in

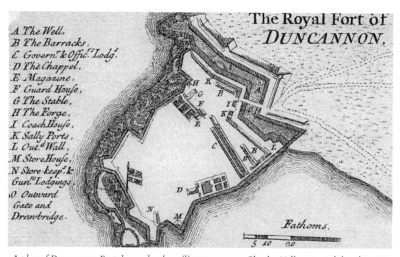

A plan of Duncannon Fort drawn by the military surveyor Charles Vallancey and dated 1759.

the New Geneva Barracks near Crooke. The camp was so named for a planned colony of Protestant asylum seekers fleeing the failed Geneva Revolution of 1782 in the small Swiss city state, but they never arrived. Prisoners at Geneva Barracks faced trial for membership of the United Irishmen and were held in squalid, overcrowded conditions, some awaiting transportation abroad. The rebel leader Thomas Cloney described it as 'the filthiest, most damp and loathsome prison, devoid of any comfort'.

The United Irishmen were sometimes referred to as 'Croppies' because many of them had their hair cropped in the style of the French Revolutionaries to show their allegiance to the rebellion. In the folk song 'The Croppy Boy', written in 1845 by the poet William B. McBurney to commemorate the Wexford Rising, one version of the last verse goes:

> 'It was in Duncannon this young man died
> And in Duncannon his body lies
> All you good people that do pass by
> Pray the Lord have mercy on the Croppy Boy'.

The strategic importance of the fort was recognized by Napoleon in the 19th century when he got intelligence on its defences in case of a French invasion of Ireland.

20TH CENTURY AND TODAY

When British rule in Ireland ended in 1922, the fort was handed over to the Free State army but during the Civil War that followed, a substantial part of it was destroyed. The fort lay in a disused state until the outbreak of World War II in 1939, when it was partially rebuilt and occupied again by the Irish army. In 1947, when the FCA army reserve was established, they used the fort mostly as a training centre until 1986. It was handed to Wexford County Council and the Office of Public Works in 1993.

The fort was used as the location for a number of key scenes in the 2002 remake of the film *The Count of Monte Cristo*, starring Richard Harris, when it was transformed into a 19th century French fortress.

Duncannon Fort is now a visitor attraction and guided tours of the 450-year-old fort are available daily in the summer months.

Victoria Cross for soldier who later joined IRA intelligence

Sergeant Major Martin Doyle from New Ross.

THE ONLY Irishman to be awarded both a Victoria Cross from Britain and a War of Independence medal from the Irish Free State was Wexfordman Martin Doyle.

Martin was born in Gusserane, near Campile, on 25 October 1894, the only son of farmer Larry Doyle and his wife Bridget. While he was still a young boy, the family moved to Mary Street in New Ross. He had six sisters and did well at school. Just two months after his 15th birthday, on St. Stephen's Day 1909, he joined the British army, claiming to be 17 at the time. His father was unhappy with his decision and so he sold a cow in order to raise the money to buy his son's way out of the armed forces. But Martin re-enlisted.

He signed up at Kilkenny Barracks as a private in the 18th Royal Irish Regiment, which recruited largely from counties Kilkenny, Wexford, Waterford and Tipperary, and was first posted to India. Martin was ambitious and enrolled in courses and night classes and took a keen interest in sports. In 1913, he became the regiment's Lightweight Boxing Champion.

At the outbreak of the First World War in 1914, Doyle returned to Ireland and, now aged 19, headed for the battlefields of France with the Royal Dublin Fusiliers. His leadership skills were soon recognized and in 1915 he was promoted to Sergeant. He rose through the ranks to Company Sergeant Major and was transferred to the Royal Munster Fusiliers.

In March 1918 he was awarded the Military Medal for bravery in battle while serving at Hattenville in Normandy. As Doyle's unit advanced towards the trenches outside Hattenville, they had come under sustained machine-gun fire from German troops holed up in a derelict barn. He led a bayonet charge and, on reaching the barn alone, routed the Germans, seized the machine-gun and took possession of the barn. He was later captured and roughly treated but his regiment secured his release following a successful counter-attack.

Six months later, on 2 September, he displayed even greater bravery near Riencourt in the Somme. For these accomplishments the Wexfordman became one of only 27 Irishmen born in what is now the Republic to be awarded the Victoria Cross in the course of WWI, Britain's premier award for gallantry 'in the presence of the enemy'. The official announcement read:

'When command of the company devolved upon him consequent upon officer casualties, and observing that some of his men were surrounded by the enemy, he led a party to their assistance, and by skilled leadership worked his way along the trenches, killed several of the enemy and extricated the party and carried back, under heavy fire, a wounded officer to a place of safety. Later seeing a tank in difficulties, he rushed forward again under intense fire, routed the German troops, who were attempting to commandeer it, and prevented the advance of another German party. A German machine gun now opened fire on the tank at close range, rendering it impossible to get the wounded away, whereupon Doyle, with great gallantry, rushed forward, and single-handed silenced the machine gun, capturing it with three prisoners. He then carried a wounded man to safety under very heavy fire. Later in the day when the enemy counter-attacked his position, he showed great power of command, driving back the enemy and capturing many prisoners. Throughout the whole of these operations, Doyle set the very highest example to all ranks by his courage and total disregard of danger.'

Sergeant Major Martin Doyle being greeted by Queen Mary at Buckingham Palace on 8 May 1919, before being decorated with both the Victoria Cross and the Military Medal by King George V, who is standing next to her.

Martin Doyle returned to New Ross after the war ended. A cheering crowd welcomed him at the train station in March 1919 and the town was decorated with bunting and banners bearing the words 'Welcome to the New Ross Hero'. Two months later, Martin travelled to Buckingham Palace, where he was decorated with the Victoria Cross and Military Medal by King George V.

But the War of Independence (1919-21) between the IRA and British forces was raging in Ireland at this time. Shortly after Martin returned from the ceremony in London he left the British army, having served for more than nine years, and joined the newly-formed IRA.

In November 1919, he married Charlotte Kennedy of New Ross and they settled in the town and went on to have a family of three daughters.

Martin became an IRA intelligence officer and in 1920 and 1921 he served in East Clare and, at considerable risk to himself, supplied arms and ammunition to the local Volunteers. While he was secretly serving in the IRA in 1920, *The Times* of London reported that he was one of the recipients of the Victoria Cross who formed part of a guard of honour at the interment of the Unknown Warrior, an unknown British soldier who was exhumed in Flanders. The ceremony took place in Westminster Abbey on 11 November 1920, the day the Cenotaph in London was unveiled by King George V.

Following the signing of the Anglo-Irish Treaty in December 1921 and the subsequent outbreak of the Civil War, Martin joined the Free State Army, who were pro-Treaty, and he served in Waterford, South Tipperary and Kilkenny (his old British Army station). When the Civil War ended in 1923, Doyle was posted back to New Ross for a short time. In 1929, he attended a Victoria Cross reunion dinner in the Royal Gallery of the House of Lords in London.

The headstone over the grave of Martin Doyle in Grangegorman Military Cemetery, Dublin.

Having spent over fifteen years in the Irish Army, he retired in 1937 but spent a further year and a half in the Dublin Army Reserve, finally giving up army life in 1939, just months before the outbreak of World War II.

The Irish Army had no pension scheme at the time when he secured a pensionable job as a security officer with Guinness Brewery in Dublin. Sadly, he died in Dublin a year later of polio, aged only 46. Although he had fought against the British and spent most of his career in the Irish Army, he was buried in Grangegorman Military Cemetery, a British Army burial ground near the Phoenix Park in Dublin. His headstone, paid for by his old WWI comrades, bears the badge of the Royal Munster Fusiliers and carries the inscription: 'Coy. Sgt. Major Martin Doyle V.C., M.M. Royal Munster Fusiliers died 20th Nov. 1940. Erected by his old comrades in the regiment'. In 1941 the Irish government issued a medal for those who served in the War of Independence but Martin Doyle did not live to receive it in person.

Doyle's Victoria Cross was purchased at auction in 1995 and is on display as part of the 'Extraordinary Heroes Exhibition' in the Imperial War Museum, London. But he is unlikely to be remembered with total pride in British military history.

The story of Martin Doyle is just one of many of the shifting loyalties and contradictions of Irish people during the turbulent period of 1919-23 that led to Irish freedom.

On Armistice Day, 11 November 2018, the 100th anniversary of the end of WWI, a plaque dedicated to Doyle was unveiled in the Tholsel, the New Ross Municipal District building. Over 870 Wexford people died in the war, many of whom have no known burial ground. Their records can be accessed at wexfordgreatwardead.ie

Farmer who gave shelter to ten evicted families

Michael Kavanagh, with his 4-year-old son Michael on his lap, sitting next to his parents and over thirty of the seventy evicted neighbours who had taken shelter on their holding in Croghan, Ballyfad on the Brooke Estate in 1887.

THE KAVANAGHS were tenants on the Brooke Estate in north County Wexford. In 1887, about sixty families, over 300 people, were evicted for refusing to pay exorbitant rent increases demanded by their landlord but the Kavanaghs were spared due to the poor health of 87-year-old Michael Kavanagh. However his son, also Michael, gave shelter to ten families, about 70 people, in outhouses on their farm.

Sir George Frederick Brooke was born in 1849 to Francis Brooke and Henrietta Monck. He lived at Summerton, Castleknock in Co. Dublin and also at Ballyfad House, Coolgreany, Co. Wexford. He was the proprietor of George F. Brooke and Son, wine merchants, and Director and Governor of the Bank of Ireland. He was also High Sheriff of Wexford in 1882 as well as High Sheriff of County Dublin in 1898 and Justice of the Peace for County Wexford and County Dublin. He had nine children from two marriages.

The Brooke Estate was located at Coolgreany, close to the border with County Wicklow. Many of its tenants struggled to pay unjustifiably high rent rises demanded by Brooke in the 1880s.

The Irish National Land League was founded in 1879 by Michael Davitt. His own family had been evicted from their home in County Mayo when their rent fell into arrears in 1850, which forced them to emigrate to England to seek a better life. Davitt became politically active, joined the Irish Republican Brotherhood and spent seven years in Dartmoor Prison, accused of treason, before returning to his native Mayo. He formed the Land League in Castlebar with Charles Stewart Parnell as president. They sought reductions in rents and fought evictions but denounced violence. During

Michael Davitt, founder of the Land League in 1879. He lost his right arm as an 11-year-old child labourer in an English cotton mill while operating a spinning machine.

the 'Land War', an English land agent in Co. Mayo called Captain Charles Boycott was ostracized by the community. He finally abandoned Ireland and this affair gave the English language the word 'boycott'. Davitt travelled to the United States to raise funds for the League with William Redmond (remembered in Redmond Park in Wexford), who was a brother of the politician John Redmond.

The Land League put forward a 'Plan of Campaign' for the tenants of the Brooke Estate in Coolgreany. The plan included withholding payment to the landlord until a rent reduction was agreed. A fund was set up into which they could pay their rent and this would be used to erect shelters called 'campaign huts' on the land of charitable neighbours, including the Kavanagh family. In December 1886, the tenants took up the call to resist Brooke's rent increases, that were impossible to meet, by issuing this statement: 'We declare our undying resolve to refuse to pay unjust exorbitant rent whilst at the same time declaring our readiness to pay that rent which the immense fall in the value of produce enable us to pay.'

In 1887, Captain Edward Hamilton, who managed the Brooke Estate and represented the Property Defence Association, began his campaign of eviction of those refusing to pay. He arrived under the protection of about a hundred police constables accompanied by twelve 'emergency men' to carry out the evictions. On 7 July, eight farmers were evicted in the Ballyfad area. Despite having rotten eggs thrown at this 'crowbar brigade', Patrick Kehoe, his wife and five young daughters were evicted from their house, followed by Thomas and Owen Kennedy from theirs and Michael Kehoe, whose house stood on 33 acres of mountain land. Farmers Daniel McDonald and Matt Redmond were also ejected from their holdings. Early the following morning, 8 July, Captain Hamilton and the emergency men arrived at the home of Patrick Greene. They were met with pots of boiling gruel being poured on them from the upstairs windows but the Greene family were evicted along with their neighbour Thomas Kinsella.

The next house they arrived at was that of Michael Kavanagh and his family in Croghan. But Michael managed to get a doctor in Arklow to certify his 87-year-old father, Michael Snr., to be unfit to move out and so their eviction did not go ahead. Michael converted outbuildings on the farm into dwellings, adding fireplaces and chimneys, for ten of the evicted families from the area, whom he invited to move into the temporary accommodation.

The 'crowbar brigade' travelled up the slopes of Croghan to the farm of William Graham. A long struggle ensued with the Grahams, who poured boiling water on the bailiffs from upstairs. Finally, the emergency men forced entry through the roof by removing slates and cutting their way in. The four Graham brothers and William's daughter and niece were all taken away in handcuffs to Wexford Jail. Next to be evicted from their holdings were John Butler of Rathpierce and Edward Mulligan, Philip Maher, and Mick Kinsella of Croghan. The last eviction in Ballyfad was later in July when a large crowd gathered outside the home of 80-year-old widow Mrs Anne D'Arcy and her daughter Catherine. Although confined to bed, Mrs D'Arcy was

Mrs. Anne D'Arcy with her daughter Catherine awaiting eviction from their home in Ballyfad, Coolgreany in July 1887.

The eviction of Mrs Anne D'Arcy. The photograph shows armed RIC constables on the left standing behind leading nationalists Michael Davitt (in light-coloured suit), Daniel Crilly MP and John Dillon MP. To their right are Fr William O'Neill, PP Killinierin, and Captain Hamilton is in the bowler hat.

defiant, telling Captain Hamilton: 'You may cast me out on the dunghill or put a bullet through my heart but death before dishonour.' The eviction was postponed, but not for long. Michael Davitt himself, along with leading nationalists John Dillon MP and Daniel Crilly MP, were present at the eviction, which was enforced by a number of armed members of the Royal Irish Constabulary.

In September, two months after their first attempt to evict the Kavanaghs and the ten families they were sheltering, Captain Hamilton took a legal case against them in an effort to remove the 'campaign huts'. As reported in the *Irish Times*, Hamilton described the huts as 'an interference with the agricultural character of the land' and he stated that the tenants were 'unpleasant to him, and that his great object was to get rid of the nuisance of the people in these huts.'

On 28 September, bailiff George Freeman, accompanied by seventeen emergency men armed with rifles and revolvers, returned to Michael Kavanagh's farm. The evicted tenants, who were still living in the outhouses and 'campaign huts', gathered inside the farmyard gate to observe the proceedings. The leader of the emergency men, John McCabe, asked to speak with Michael Kavanagh, claiming he had a warrant to seize property to the

Some of the tenants who were evicted from the Brooke Estate, including John Tierney (bottom left) who built the 'campaign huts'.

value of £57 in lieu of unpaid rents. Kavanagh came forward and demanded to first see the warrant but McCabe was unable to produce it. When one of the emergency men, John 'Red' Johnston, tried to climb the gate, one of the evicted tenants, John Kinsella, struck the gate with a pitchfork. George Freeman immediately produced his revolver and shot dead the 64-year-old widower and father of four children – Patrick, Myles, Elizabeth and Bridget – while the emergency men fired over the heads of the crowd. As his corpse was being taken inside the house, the emergency men saw their opportunity and seized fourteen cows from the property.

At the inquest into the death of John Kinsella, the verdict stated: 'We find that the said John Kinsella came by his death at Coolgreany, in the county of Wexford, on the 28th September 1887 by a gunshot wound inflicted feloniously, maliciously, and of malice aforethought, by George Freeman, aided and abetted by John McCabe, ... John Johnston (Red) ... and E.C. Hamilton.' Captain Hamilton and a number of other men were released on bail but Freeman and nine others were held in custody in Wexford Jail. In the subsequent murder trial all were acquitted. Defiant Michael Kavanagh later took a case against George Brooke for the wrongful removal of his cattle, which he won.

Brooke found new tenants for the vacant holdings but they were boycotted by the local community and left the area after a few years. It was not until the Wyndham Land Act of 1903 that the Irish land question was successfully addressed. A new scheme was worked out for tenants to purchase land, with the government paying the difference between the price offered by tenants and that demanded

Michael Kavanagh with his children Margaret and Michael and his parents outside their farmhouse in Croghan, Ballyfad.

by landlords. By 1914, threequarters of tenants in the country had purchased the titles to the land that they occupied. Many of the evicted tenants, some of whom had been staying in Gorey and Arklow, returned to their homes in the Coolgreany area following the change in the law.

Brooke's son Lieutenant George Brooke and his wife Nina Hill lived in Ballyfad House from the time they married in 1907. But Lt. Brooke was killed in France in WWI and in 1919 the 'Trinity Window' in the Protestant church in Inch was added by the Brooke family in his memory. Sir George Frederick Brooke died in 1926.

The remarkable photographs featured here come from an album held in the National Library of Ireland. It was compiled by a T. Mallacy (presumably the photographer) in 1887 and presented the following year to Father Laurence Farrelly, who was himself active in the 'Plan of Campaign' in County Wexford at the time. Father Farrelly's grand-niece in Australia, Mrs Brigid Hogan, gifted this copy of the album to the library in 1992. A similar album, which was saved from a fire in 1926, was donated to the National Museum in 1942.

At the gate of the Kavanagh's farm where John Kinsella was shot dead. Michael Kavanagh stands to the left of young women who had been incarcerated in Wexford Jail for pouring boiling water on the 'emergency men'.

Reclaiming land between the sea and coastal Bridgetown

The Cull Bank sea wall and pumphouse. Ballyteige Lough is on the left and the reclaimed slobland on the right with Carrigbyrne Hill in the distance. (photo: Des Kiely)

UNTIL the mid-1800s the land from Cullenstown to Bridgetown and Kilmore village flooded at high tide, making it accessible to small shipping vessels from the sea as far as both villages. An extract from *A Topographical Dictionary of Ireland* by Samuel Lewis published in 1837: 'Kilmore... is situated on the eastern shore of the lough formed by the burrow of Ballyteigue, a long narrow sand bank extending from Ballyteigue for nearly four Irish miles, to the entrance of the lake at its western extremity...'

John Rowe of Ballycross House, one-time High Sheriff of County Wexford, instigated the draining of the submerged land and was one of a syndicate of local landowners behind the scheme. The Rowe family, who were granted lands near Bridgetown in the mid-1600s following the Cromwellian campaign, were one of the largest landowners in the area with about 8,000 acres. John Rowe built Ballycross House in about 1837. (The house was demolished in 1948 and rebuilt and, following a fire, a new house was constructed in the early 1960s by the Von Engelbrechten family from Germany, who later established Ballycross Apple Farm). Ebenezer Rowe built Rowe Street in Wexford town where the family had their townhouse, which later became the offices of Huggard & Brennan solicitors.

In 1844 the Board of Public Works published a report entitled *Proposed Drainage of the Flooded Lands in the District of Ballyteige*, proposing 'cutting and sinking a navigable canal from tideway at Blackstone to the village of Bridgetown.' They planned on draining most of the submerged land by building a dam on Ballyteige Lough at Cull Bank, Ballyteige Burrow and digging a canal system linking the Lough with Bridgetown, which was then

This detail from a 1685 map of County Wexford shows how land flooded at high tide from Cullenstown to Bridgetown and close to Kilmore village. Engraved by William Petty, who was an English economist, physician and cartographer. Two years after Cromwell left Ireland, Petty arrived in 1652 as physician-general to Cromwell's army. He was also tasked with surveying the land that was to be confiscated and given to Cromwell's soldiers. Between 1654 and 1656 he charted the entire country (known as the 'Down Survey' because the results were set down in maps). In return Petty was paid £9,000 and given 3,500 acres in 'Kilmare' (now Kenmare), Co. Kerry.

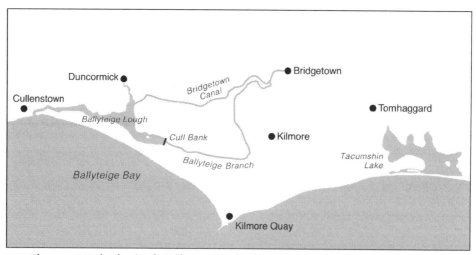

The same area today showing the Bridgetown Canal and Ballyteige Branch connecting Bridgetown and Ballyteige Lough or Cull Pond. © Des Kiely

coastal. There were objections to the scheme from local landowners, fishermen and merchants, who stood to lose access to the sea by ship.

The subsequent construction work acted as a relief measure for the poor, giving employment to thousands of men at the time of the Great Famine of 1845-49. Some men walked up to twelve miles to work on the scheme and back home again at the end of the day.

The Cull Bank, an earthen dam, was faced with limestone blocks sourced from the nearby Seafield quarry. The wall initially had four sluice gates, which were opened on the falling tide. But today the Cull Pumphouse, operated by the OPW, continuously drains water from the polder land back into the lagoon. The construction of the dam resulted in the creation of the Inish and Ballyteige Slob, which consists of about 1,800 acres of reclaimed land. The shallow Ballyteige Lough, known locally as Bar o' Lough, extends from the sea at Cullenstown to Duncormick and now ends at the Cull Bank.

In order to facilitate shipping beyond Duncormick to Bridgetown, the five-mile-long Bridgetown Canal was built between 1850 and 1853, linking Ballyteige Lough at Blackstone, near Duncormick, via Yoletown and Bridgetown. The Ballyteige navigable branch forked off and ran directly to the Cull Bank. A further thousand acres of low-lying farmland in the Mayglass-

The four-arch humpback bridge over Bridgetown Canal in the village of Bridgetown. (photo: Des Kiely)

Bridgetown area that had been liable to flooding could now be drained into the canal.

Two quays were constructed in Bridgetown and landing slips were provided at points along the canal. Coal was imported from South Wales by small vessels that returned with grain or potatoes and the

The canal linking Bridgetown with Ballyteigue, dug by manual labour, photographed in 1935. (photo: Albert Eskeröd/Dúchas)

canal continued in use for about 90 years until the 1940s. The railway connecting Rosslare and Waterford came to Bridgetown in 1906 with the opening of Bridgetown station but the service ceased in 2010.

Until recently, one crafty resident of Bridgetown made use of the canal by travelling by boat to Sammy Sinnott's Bar in Duncormick for his regular few pints, thereby circumventing the drink driving regulations.

The polder land, in part reminiscent of a landscape in Holland, is scattered with attractive small cut-limestone bridges that cross Bridgetown Canal and the Ballyteige Branch, some of which can be seen when driving the road from Baldwinstown to Kilmore Quay.

Ballycross House, the home of John Rowe, was built c.1837 and demolished following a fire in 1948. A new house was built in its place by the Von Engelbrechten family in the 1960s.

100 killed in 'The First Wexford Rebellion' in 1793

(From an original drawing by Edward Seibert)

IN the early 1790s there were rumblings of discontent throughout County Wexford. Sectarian tensions combined with hostility to the brutal public executions and burning of homes by Crown forces. Conservative Protestants were actively recruiting for the Wexford militia in response to the growing unrest but liberal Protestants such as Cornelius Grogan of Johnstown Castle were against the formation of the militia. The United Irishmen were formed in 1790 in Belfast and Dublin, and membership was growing nationwide.

Catholics were protesting against the enforced payment of tithes to the Anglican Church; both Catholics and Presbyterians were obliged to hand over one-tenth of their crops and annual earnings to the clergy. On Monday, 8 July 1793, a crowd of rebels assembled at Templescoby, two miles outside Enniscorthy on the New Ross road, to protest against the tax. Two Bunclody men, who were carrying arms, were arrested and taken to Wexford Jail, then located in Stafford's Castle on South Main Street, between Oyster Lane and Stonebridge.

On the following Thursday, 11 July, an anonymous letter was received by the town magistrates demanding the release of the prisoners. It also contained a threat that if this was refused, a force of 3,000 rebels would march on Wexford and burn the town to the ground. The threat was not taken seriously until at three o'clock word reached the military barracks that a huge force of insurgents armed with pikes, scythes and guns were approaching. Along the way they had captured a redcoat, a Lieutenant Buckby, and taken him along as a hostage.

A force of about fifty soldiers led by Major Charles Vallotton, a veteran of the Spanish Wars, and Lieutenant Colonel Oliver Nicholl marched towards John Street to prevent the 'mob' entering the town.

The two groups met at the north end of John Street, close to the Hill Street junction. Vallotton went forward to speak with the apparent leader of the group, 22-year-old John Moore from Robinstown near Old Ross, who carried a scythe across his shoulder. When Vallotton caught sight of Buckby, who was being held by the crowd, he became enraged and struck Moore with his sword. Moore in turn swept his scythe into Vallotton's groin. Both men collapsed and the military at once started firing on the crowd. As the protesters scattered, eleven were shot dead on the spot on John Street. Hundreds fled for their lives out of town along what is now Newtown Road, but Wexford militia officer

Captain James Boyd and his men, who were returning from patrol, were lying in ambush. They shot dead about eighty protesters at Bettyville (now the location of Wexford Racecourse).

Eight protesters were found hiding in a hayloft on John Street. One died from his wounds, two turned informer and five were later put on trial. The five, James Kenney, Patrick Flannery, Patrick Neil, Michael Carty and John Crawford, were hanged on nearby Windmill Hill (Belvedere Road) on 26 July. Both John Moore and Major Vallotton died from their wounds but Lieutenant Buckby had escaped. John Moore is buried at Carnagh, Ballinaboola.

The Vallotton monument at Wygram in Wexford town, looking towards Hill Street and John Street junction, was hastily erected by Wexford Corporation in 1794. (photo: Wexford County Library)

The following year Wexford Corporation, in an effort to show loyalty to the British forces, erected an obelisk to Vallotton close to the location of the killings: at Wygram near the junction of John Street and Newtown Road.

According to the Corporation's minutes of 30 December 1793 it was agreed that '...a monument be erected in the church of the town, and a monumental obelisk raised on the spot where he was killed at the expense of the Corporation to the late Major Charles Vallotton of the 56th regiment of Infantry who fell in the defence of the town of Wexford, when attacked by a dangerous and riotous mob, and that the Burgesses now present or any five of them be a committee to determine on the plan, inscription and expense thereof.' The inscription on the obelisk, now barely legible, reads:

'To the memory of Major Charles Vallotton murdered at Wexford in Ireland
July 11 1793 whilst in the act of expostulating with a lawless mob'.

The Corporation also installed a memorial plaque to Vallotton in St. Iberius

Church with the following elaborate inscription:

> '*Sacred to the memory of the late Charles Vallotton Esqr.*
>
> *A Major in the Army & a Capt. in the 56th Regt. of Infantry Who in the Suburbs on the 11th of July 1793 when zealously co-opperating with the Civil Power in support of the mild & beneficent laws of his Country received a mortal Wound from a savage Hand. Thus untimely fell this accomplish'd Gentleman not less admir'd & belov'd for every social quality than he was eminently distinguish'd on every occasion by the enterprize and galantry of a Soldier. Reader lament with every good Man the irreperable Loss & strive to emulate his many Virtues. The Corporation of Wexford with becoming Gratitude erected this monument to perpetuate their high respect for his inestimable Character.'*

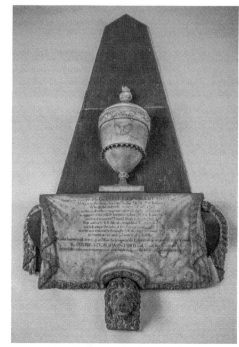

Memorial in St. Iberius Church to Charles Vallotton. *(photo: Des Kiely)*

Lieutenant Colonel Oliver Nicholl, commander of the 45th regiment, was presented by the Corporation of Wexford with a gold medal for services rendered. It had the arms and motto of the town of Wexford on one side and on the reverse the following inscription:

> '*Dedicated to Oliver Nicholls, Lieut.-Colonel of the 45th regiment, by the inhabitants of Wexford, armed to protect the peace thereof, against the insults of an armed mob which appeared before its walls, 11th July, 1793, as a testimonial of their gratitude justly due to his distinguished aid and active zeal in co-operating with them.'*

A plaque dedicated to John Moore and the other victims was more recently placed at the intersection of Belvedere Road and Newtown Road, opposite the Vallotton obelisk and reads:

'In commemoration of John Moore of Robinstown who on 11th July, 1793 at the age of 22 led 2,000 men to this town to rescue comrades from Wexford gaol. Challenged here by the 45th Regiment of Infantry under Major Charles Vallotton, John Moore and some 80 people were killed in the ensuing conflict. Five men were arrested and executed. Their memory endures.

Cuimhneofar ar laochóg is ar a chompánaigh mar aon leis.

(A young noble warrior will be remembered, as will his companions)'

The plaque at Wygram to John Moore and the other victims of 11 July 1793. (photo: Des Kiely)

The people of Wexford had never witnessed such violence and the town would never be the same again. The events of 11 July 1793 are often referred to as the 'First Wexford Rebellion'. Shortly after these atrocities, people began to manufacture pikes in great numbers and hid them away to guarantee some security for the people and for use in a possible future rebellion. A pike-making factory was located in the Bullring, where blacksmiths forged pikes and repaired weapons in preparation for the uprising. Spurred on by the French Revolution, which was underway, membership of the Society of the United Irishmen was rapidly growing. Their goal was the creation of a non-sectarian Irish republic, independent from Britain and to be achieved by armed rebellion. Following the collapse in grain prices in 1797 due to the imposition of new taxes and the resulting hardship in the county, the rebellion in Wexford finally came in 1798.

According to Wexford Borough Council meeting minutes from 1997 it was proposed to rededicate the Vallotton monument to all the victims of the 1793 Rebellion, reflecting both traditions. Today the inscription on the obelisk remains illegible; it is believed that people entering the town for years threw stones at it to obliterate the wording and spat on it as they passed.

In memory of Wexford soldiers killed in the Crimean War

The Crimean Monument above Ferrycarrig Bridge, early 1900s. (photo: National Library of Ireland)

THE ROUND tower at Ferrycarrig, unveiled in 1858, was built as a memorial to the Wexford casualties of the Crimean War that ended just two years earlier. The war claimed the lives of nearly 7,000 Irish who fought on the side of Britain against the Russian Empire.

In 1853 Russia declared war on the Ottoman-Turkish Empire, in part over the rights of Christian minorities in the Holy Land. France, Britain and Sardinia-Piedmont promised to support Turkey in what became known as the Crimean War.

In the early months of 1854 Ireland was gripped by a kind of war fever as young men rushed to join up, the war coming so soon after the Famine. Public enthusiasm bordered on hysteria as the troops left for the East. The Irish made up about one third of the British army at the time and around 30,000 Irish soldiers served in the war against Russia. In February 1854, the 50th Foot Regiment, commanded by Wexford-born Lt. Col. Richard Waddy, was one of the first regiments to leave Dublin for battle. Many Irish doctors, nurses, priests and policemen volunteered to go to Crimea to help in the war effort. Irish engineers and navvies worked on new roads and railways and the Crimean War was the first conflict to be covered by war correspondents, who operated without restrictions imposed by any form of censorship. The most prominent was Dublin-born William Russell, who wrote for *The Times* of London and exposed the British army's lack of organization.

The Lord Lieutenant of Ireland, the Earl of Carlisle, George Howard, laid the foundation stone of the Crimean Monument at Carrig.

The majority of the British 21,000 fatal casualties died from disease, and only 4,700 were killed in action. Almost 7,000 Irish soldiers died in the conflict. The war ended in an Allied victory and the Treaty of Paris in 1856.

The conclusion of the war was celebrated in Ireland at the Great Crimean Banquet, which took place in the Tobacco Stores, a bonded warehouse on Customs House Docks, Dublin, on the 22 October 1856. Five thousand

The civic ceremony at Carrig on 8 October 1857. It was attended by the Lord Lieutenant of Ireland, who travelled to Wexford from his residence in the Phoenix Park, the Viceregal Lodge, now Áras an Uachtaráin.

victorious soldiers, seamen and guests gathered. Over £3,600 was raised by public subscription to cover the cost of what must surely have been the largest ever formal dinner in Ireland. Three tons of hot potatoes were sent in four vans, which pulled up to the hall 'steaming like locomotives'. A vast amount of food and drink was consumed, including 250 hams, 230 legs of mutton, 500 meat pies, 100 venison pasties, 100 rice puddings, 260 plum puddings, 200 turkeys, 200 geese, 250 joints of beef, 100 chickens, and 2,000 two-pound loaves. Each serviceman was given a quart of porter and a pint of port or sherry. Considering this was just seven years after the Famine, such a lavish celebration is impressive.

Soon thereafter monuments were erected across Ireland to remember those who were lost in the war.

A committee headed by Lord Carew of Castleboro House, Clonroche (later

The Crimean Monument stands on a promontory above the River Slaney and was completed in 1858 on the site of the first Anglo-Norman castle ever built in Ireland in 1169. (photo: Des Kiely)

burnt to the ground by the IRA in an arson attack in 1923), was set up in Wexford to build a memorial to the men of Wexford who died. A total of £300 was collected by public subscription and the County Surveyor, Edwin Willis of Rowe Street, came up with the round tower design. A contemporary of the Crimean Monument was the memorial to Daniel O'Connell, also in the form of a round tower, which was erected in Glasnevin Cemetery three years earlier in 1855. O'Connell's remains were exhumed and reinterred in a crypt beneath the tower in 1869.

Lord Donoughmore (Richard Hely-Hutchinson) donated this famous piece of headland at Carrig overlooking the Slaney. A civic ceremony was held at the site on 8 October 1857 and the foundation stone for the war memorial was laid by the Lord Lieutenant of Ireland, the Earl of Carlisle.

The first Norman castle built in Ireland was constructed at this spot by Robert FitzStephen, the leader of the Anglo-Normans who landed at Bannow Island in 1169. After the fall of Wexford, he sited what is classified as a ringwork castle in this strategic location known as Carrig in the winter of 1169, a year before the main Anglo-Norman landing party arrived at Baginbun. The medieval town of Carrig, consisting of over a hundred houses, developed around the hilltop fort and survived for about 130 years before falling into ruin. This new borough area on the southern side of the Slaney gave the townland the name Newtown, although it is commonly referred to as Ferrycarrig ('the ferry to Carrig'), which lies on the northern side of the river.

An archaeological site study was carried out ahead of the building of the new N11 road in the early 1980s. Further excavations at the site were started in 2018 and may continue for many years. A 12th century ditch, two metres deep, and a defence wall have been exposed. The remains of 12th century wooden structures represent some of the very first Anglo-Norman constructions in the country.

Stone from Carrig Castle was collected and used in the building of the Crimean Monument. A replica of the original Norman castle was erected close to the site, which now forms part of the Irish National Heritage Park. The park opened in 1987 following the construction of the N11 road as an open-air museum. It tells the story of human settlement in Ireland from the Mesolithic period right up to the Norman Invasion.

The round tower memorial was completed in 1858 and a leaden case was buried in the base of the tower, containing a copy of a newspaper of the day, the list of subscribers and some coins of the period. The marble plaque at the base was added in 1868 and reads: 'In memory of the officers, non commissioned officers and men of the County Wexford who lost their lives in the Crimea during the war with Russia 1854-56.'

The Nation newspaper (once edited by Wexfordwoman Jane Elgee, mother of Oscar Wilde) denounced the tower as 'another monument commemorative of British rule in Ireland that would offer the commemorated soldier's mother no solace should she be evicted when she became unable to pay her rent to the loss of her son who had taken the Saxon shilling.'

BROWNE-CLAYTON MONUMENT

Visible from the Wexford to New Ross road near Carrigbyrne, stands another 19th century tower monument, dedicated to Sir Ralph Abercromby on Carrigadaggan Hill. Completed in 1841, seventeen years before the Crimean Monument, it commemorates the army officer who was victorious in Napoleon's campaign in Egypt but died in the Battle of Alexandria in 1801. It was commissioned by General Robert Browne-Clayton (*d.*1845), who fought under Abercromby and married Henrietta Clayton in 1803. Abercromby was Commander-in-Chief of the British forces in Ireland in 1798.

The 94-foot-high (28-metre) Browne-Clayton Monument was completed in 1841. (photo: Des Kiely)

The Browne family came to Ireland with Cromwell's army in 1649. Browne's Hill, a Georgian mansion near Carlow town, was built in 1763 on the site of the ancient abbey of St. Kieran. The house was completely redesigned in 1830 by the architect Thomas Cobden, who also designed Carlow Cathedral, Duckett's Grove and later the Browne-Clayton Monument.

The column was based on the 20-metre Pompey's Pillar near Alexandria, which Abercromby would have seen for the first time on the day he was killed. It is the only internally accessible Corinthian column in existence, having an internal stairway. It was constructed by James Johnston of Carlow over two years and was built using Mount Leinster granite.

In 1994, when the column was struck by lightning, a large gaping hole was made in the top section and the internal stairway was blocked by falling debris. A trust was formed in 2001 with the objectives of acquiring, restoring and repairing the monument. The land on which it is situated was purchased by the trust and a direct access pathway from the public road was acquired. The restoration work was completed in 2003.

Known locally as 'Browne's Nonsense', legend has it that Browne originally built it in memory of his son, who was thought to have been killed in battle, but who turned up alive and well shortly after completion of the monument.

Brutal murder of sweet shop owner in Cinema Lane

The entrance to Cinema Lane or Harper's Lane from South Main Street, and inset: the victim William Hannan. On the left is Eddie Hall's public house, formerly the Cinema Bar once owned and operated by William.
(Main photo: John Scanlon)

WEXFORD TOWN had three cinemas in the 1950s. The Capitol Cinema on South Main Street opened in 1931 and operated until 1984; it was demolished and the new building is now occupied by Colman Doyle Home Store. The Abbey Cinema was located on George's Street and opened in 1947. The site is now occupied by an apartment block called Abbey Court. The first cinema in the town was the Cinema Palace, converted from an old warehouse in 1914 in Harper's Lane, also known as Cinema Lane.

Harper's Lane is believed to have been named after Francis Harper, three times mayor of Wexford: in 1834, 1835 and 1839. He owned businesses that occupied almost every building in the lane from South Main Street to Crescent Quay. Curiously the name is translated literally on the street nameplate as 'Cúlán an Chlairseóra' or *Harpist's Lane*. The lane was previously known as Hay's Lane and Moran's Lane but today is still called Cinema Lane locally, despite the cinema closing its doors in 1970.

Although sweets and soft drinks were available in the Cinema Palace, there was a bigger selection to be had in *The Dainty* sweet shop in the lane. The popular shop was run by William Hannan, originally from Crecora near Limerick city, who lived just 50 yards away at 70 South Main Street (now Lotus House). He was married to local woman Margaret Moran, they had three grown-up children and William was a resident of the town for over thirty years.

William, an unassuming, religious and well-educated man, had studied in All Hallows College in Dublin and in UCD. He interrupted his course in UCD to join the RAF during World War I before coming to Wexford in 1919, where he attended St. Peter's College for three years. He then taught for the following three years at a grammar school in Shoreham in Essex before returning to Wexford in 1925.

William purchased Codd's grocery and spirits shop on the corner of South Main Street and Cinema Lane (now occupied by Costa Coffee). He operated a licensed premises, the Cinema Bar, here as well as *The Dainty* sweet shop adjoining the property around the corner in the narrow laneway. In 1954, William relinquished the licensed trade and let the business to local town councillor and former Mayor of Wexford, Eddie Hall (the maternal grandfather of Councillor George Lawlor). But he continued to operate the sweet shop mainly to cater for cinemagoers.

William's practice was to open his shop every night for people going to the nearby Cinema Palace, which had two showings, from 7pm to 9pm and again from 9pm to 11pm. He closed during the performances and re-opened when people were leaving.

Eddie Hall was Mayor of Wexford in 1956 and 1961. He ran the pub, Eddie Hall's, formerly the Cinema Bar. (photo: John Scanlon)

Hannan was deeply interested in literature and his hobby was hand-printing, which he carried on in a room at the back of the shop, sometimes while the cinema's shows were on. He specialized in reprinting *St. Colmcille's Prophesies* under the trade name 'Unique Publications'. These sold particularly well in Ireland, Britain and the USA, providing him with an extra source of income. On the occasion of the unveiling of the John Barry statue on Crescent Quay in 1957, he wrote and published a booklet *The John Barry Story*. He was a first cousin of one of the country's leading consultant engineers, Nicholas O'Dwyer, who designed the Cusack Stand in Croke Park.

On the night of Saturday, 8 March 1958, four men were playing in a back room of Eddie Hall's pub that was separated from the sweet shop by a doorless partition. At around 10.45pm, they heard scuffling followed by moaning from next door. One of the card players, William Scanlon from nearby Henrietta Street, entered the lane and found the shop door locked. Through the glass panel on the door he could see two young men aged 20 to 22 standing in the room behind the shop where William Hannan had his printing press. When they spotted Scanlon the pair shut the door and turned off the shop lights. Scanlon banged several times on the door shouting "Open up! Open up!" but got no response. His shouts brought Eddie Hall and a number of other people to the door of the shop. They too got no reply to their knocks and so they alerted the gardaí and William's family across on South Main Street.

The gardaí, along with Hannan's 25-year-old son Patrick, entered the sweet shop by breaking the glass panel and found 65-year-old William lying unconscious on the floor in a pool of blood and moaning. His broken pipe and a number of coins were scattered on the floor. He was given the Last Rights by Fr. Matthew Doyle and taken to the County Hospital, arriving shortly after midnight. William died at 9.25am the next morning without having regained consciousness.

At first William's death was treated as a possible accident, the result of a fall from a ladder that was fixed to the wall in the back room of the shop and used to reach the loft above. But a post-mortem carried out by the State Pathologist, Dr. Maurice Hickey, revealed injuries so extensive that they pointed to having been caused by a brutal assault. He had 13 wounds to the head and injuries to the fingers on both hands, perhaps the result of trying to defend himself before he was beaten down. The weapon used was believed to have been either an iron bar or a piece of hard wood.

At about the time of the murder, a car belonging to John Cardiff of Mountpleasant, near Mayglass, had entered the water at Crescent Quay in an apparently unrelated incident. Hundreds of people and several gardaí were at the scene. People were passing up and down Cinema Lane, which leads to the Crescent Quay. When the gardaí forced their way into the sweet shop just before 11pm, people soon began streaming out of the cinema.

At 10.40pm, William Hannan had served his last customer, Mr. C. Jones, a shoemaker from Corn-market, who was on his way home from the cinema with his son when they knocked on the shop door, which was locked. Mr. Hannan let them in to buy some chewing gum.

It's believed that the assailants called to the shop immediately after that and demanded money. Having lethally assaulted William Han-

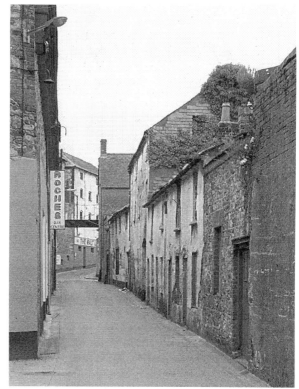

Cinema Lane, the location of William Hannan's murder. Looking up from Crescent Quay, the first building on the left was the Cinema Palace. (photo: John Scanlon)

nan, they probably used the ladder and escaped through the skylight. This was the only exit from the building apart from the front door. They must have scrambled over adjoining roofs before finally dropping into nearby Henrietta Street and heading towards Crescent Quay, where the commotion over the car in the water was under way. This would have enabled them to slip away unnoticed.

Michael Kehoe, who lived at 41 South Main Street (today part of the Mountain Warehouse shop), was disturbed by the noise of falling mortar or a brick from a wall at the rear that adjoined Cinema Lane. He heard shouting outside and caught a glimpse of coat-tails through his back window. He later learned that the shouting was from the gardaí at the sweet shop in the lane.

John Scanlon, a brother of William Scanlon (and who was the photographer who took some of the photographs in this article), left his house on John's Gate Street at 10.45pm to walk his dog. He turned into Henrietta Street at about 10.55 and spotted a young man emerge from between parked cars and the boundary wall over which the suspects are believed to have made their escape. When the man saw Scanlon, he turned around and faced the cars. John Scanlon sensed that there was a second man under the wall, though he did not see him.

A thorough search of the area was carried out by a team of about 30 gardaí and members of the Technical Bureau from Dublin. Fingerprints were taken and several people were interviewed. The descriptions of two young men aged about 22 who had left Wexford shortly after the murder and had been seen in the area at the time were circulated throughout Ireland and Britain and appeals made on radio. The gardaí subsequently found a steel bar about a foot long among the roofs over which the murderers escaped but this was later ruled out as the murder weapon.

It is believed that robbery was the motive and that the killers were disturbed before they could take much, although a tobacco box in which William was known to have kept money was missing. When he was being undressed in the hospital, £276 in cash was found in his pocket. He may have removed this from the till before he met his death. He was in the habit of carrying large sums of money with him and he also had dollars in his workshop, earned from sales of his books. Among William's manuscripts of yet-to-be-published stories found in his printing workshop was *The Legacy*, a detective story about a man who was murdered for his money.

The old Cinema Palace premises on Cinema Lane today.

South Main Street around the time of William Hannan's murder in 1958. Eddie Hall's pub was the fourth building on the left after the Temperance Hotel. Witness Michael Kehoe lived above the premises with the slate cladding next door to the hotel.

The brutal slaying of William Hannan shocked the people of the town of Wexford and caused a nationwide sensation. Six months into the investigation, the gardaí held a press conference and said: 'We never give up hope and can always wait patiently for the day when something new will crop up which will lead us to the killer or killers'. The gardaí believe that the perpetrators remained in the town and although there were suspicions cast on some locals, the case remains unsolved to this day.

Murders were rare in Ireland in the 1950s. In his book *Christine Falls*, the acclaimed Wexford-born author John Banville, who pens crime fiction books under the alias Benjamin Black, wrote:

"Even Wexford was not without its grisly glories: we were horribly thrilled when the owner of a sweet shop in Cinema Lane was bludgeoned to death one black winter night by an intruder who was never brought to justice, though everyone knew his identity. The thought of all that blood spilled among the toffee bars and the bottles of bull's-eyes was deliciously shiver-inducing. Oh, we were shocked by such excesses, of course, but as George Orwell pointed out in his essay *The Decline of the English Murder*, we all like nothing better than a good, juicy homicide."

Mysterious origin of the Doll's House in Rathaspeck

The Doll's House, a two-bedroomed gate lodge to Rathaspeck Manor, is painted a distinctive bright blue with yellow details and a red roof. (photo: Des Kiely)

LOCAL CHILDREN were once told that if they looked through its windows for long enough they would turn into dolls. The origin of the Doll's House, a gate lodge to Rathaspeck Manor, remains a mystery. Rathaspeck (in Irish: *Rath an Easpaig,* meaning Fort of the Bishop), lies about 3km southwest of Wexford town.

THE CODD FAMILY

Following the conquest of England by the Normans in 1066, families like the Codds intermarried with the French settlers. The medieval Gaelic kingdom of Uí Ceinnsialaigh (anglicized Kinsella) is now substantially represented by the present-day County Wexford. In the 12th century, Diarmait Mac Murchada, the deposed king of Uí Ceinnsialaigh and Leinster, sought aid from King Henry

II and this led to the Anglo-Norman invasion of 1169. Offers of land and increased social status were made to the English and Welsh settlers who brought with them such names as Barry, Butler, Browne, Codd, Devereux, Fitzhenry, Furlong, Hore, Lambert, Meyler, Neville, Roche, Rossiter, Stafford, Sutton and Whitty. These names continue to be strongly represented in the county.

The Codds erected tower houses in the Carne area at Ballyfane, Clougheast and Castletown and also at Ballymacane near Tacumshane. Sir Osborne Codd built a castle at Rathaspeck in 1351.

One notable member of the Codd family was Anastasia Codd, daughter of shopkeeper Thomas Codd, and a resident of Cornmarket in the centre of Wexford town. She was born in 1758 and was the mother of the bard and poet Thomas Moore. Today the house is a restaurant and bar called the Thomas Moore Tavern. A property survey from the 1800s shows that there were 159 Codd households in Wexford, far more than in any other county.

There is no longer any trace of Sir Osborne Codd's castle but it is believed that Rathaspeck Manor, built between 1680 and 1720 also by the Codd family, stands on the site of Rathaspeck Castle.

THE RICHARDS FAMILY

Jane Codd, who succeeded her father Loftus Codd of Castletown, Carne, married Thomas Richards. The Richards had come to Ireland around 1570 and Jane and Thomas inherited Rathaspeck. They had six sons and two

Rathaspeck Manor is a 300-year-old Georgian house now offering five-star accommodation and a par 3 golf course.

daughters and their first child, Thomas, was born into Rathaspeck Manor in 1722. He later married Martha Redmond and became the father of two daughters. The elder, Martha, married Count Wilmersdorf of Hanover. They had a family of three daughters and one son, another Thomas, who died unmarried in 1834. Elizabeth was born in 1778.

Aged 20 when the Rebellion broke out in 1798, Elizabeth kept a daily diary of events of the time and continued writing it until 1825. She recorded the family's real fear of being killed by the rebels in the summer of 1798. Elizabeth kept notes on the burning of Enniscorthy, the battles in New Ross, Three Rocks and Foulkesmills and the murders and executions in Wexford. She expressed her shock at the hanging on her neighbour Cornelius Grogan of nearby Johnstown Castle as well as Beauchamp Bagenal Harvey of Bargy Castle and John Henry Colclough of Ballyteigue.

She married a 27-year-old Dutch count, Frederik Willem van Limburg Stirum, in 1802 and they had ten children between 1803 and 1820, all born in Wexford. The family moved to the Nether-lands in 1821. The diary was found in 1917 by Elizabeth's granddaughter, Anna Elizabeth Groeninx van Zoelen, in Huys ten Donck, her family's seat in Ridderkerk near Rotterdam. It was published as a book in 1999 titled *The Diary of Elizabeth Richards (1798-1825): From the Wexford Rebellion in Ireland to Family Life in the Netherlands*. The original diary is held in a museum in the Netherlands.

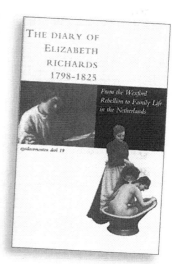

DOLL'S HOUSE

Sometime in the 19th century, an English family by the name of Moody took possession of Rathaspeck Manor. It was Edmund Moody who replaced an earlier gate lodge with the 'Doll's House' in 1900. In his 1996 book, *100 Wexford Country Houses,* Dan Walsh speculated that the house may have been a pavilion at the Paris Exposition of 1900 and was transported to Ireland at the conclusion of the fair. It was said that Moody had visited the Paris Exhibition. But another theory is that Moody might have built the timber dwelling himself locally as he was at the time the owner of a sawmill. It seems

The Doll's House interior was restored in 2017 and is available for short-term letting. (photos: Rathaspeck Manor)

the mystery of the origin of the 'Doll's House' may never be solved.

Rathaspeck Manor changed hands again in 1911 when it was purchased by the Meyler family. It transferred to the Cuddihys in 1951 and from 1969 Michael and Ella Cuddihy operated a bed-and-breakfast business. Their son Mick and his wife Betty took over the manor in 2005.

The 'Doll's House' has had many tenants over the years and the last was Mick's aunt Lil. The Victorian gate lodge has been a protected structure since 2001 and the Heritage Council part-funded the restoration, starting in 2004 when the roof and windows were replaced. The exterior woodwork was restored by the Cuddihys, who also had new wiring, plumbing and central heating installed. In 2017, the entire interior was restored and tastefully furnished and the gate lodge is now available for short-term letting.

RATHASPECK CHURCH

The village of Rathaspeck boasted its own police station in the 1800s. The present Rathaspeck Church of Ireland was built in 1823 and functioned until 1971. An extract from the 1877 *Chronicles of the County Wexford* by George Griffiths on Chapels in the Barony of Forth: 'In Rathaspocke peece, a Church dedicated to St. Bridget, patroness of Ireland. [Rathaspock, i.e. "fort of the bishop," now the parish of that name. The present church is a modern building, and was erected in 1823 at a cost of about £900, aided by a grant from the Board of First Fruits.]' The graveyard holds the remains of Cornelius Grogan, the owner of adjoining Johnstown Castle estate, who was a warden in the original church that stood on the site.

JOHNSTOWN CASTLE

With the coming of the Normans, lands later known as Johnstown were acquired by the Esmondes, who were Catholic. Oliver Cromwell's troops are said to have occupied the demesne on the night before their attack on Wexford town in October 1649, but not before expelling the Esmondes and destroying their castle. In 1692, the estate was acquired by John Grogan, a Protestant Wexford merchant of English origin. Cornelius Grogan, born in 1738, was appointed High Sheriff of Wexford in 1779 and elected MP for Enniscorthy from 1769 to 1773.

Grogan suffered from severe gout and walked slowly and with difficulty. He wore his white hair long, was a popular landlord, had liberal principles and supported reform and Catholic emancipation. He joined the United Irishmen and became one of the four members of the governing committee of the short-lived 'Wexford Republic'. He was put in charge of food supplies and had grain coming in through the south of the town.

When the United Irishmen were defeated, Grogan was arrested at Johnstown, then a tower house, on 25 June 1798. He was court-martialled in the Courthouse in the Bullring, found guilty of complicity in the insurrection and was marched down the Main Street to Wexford Jail. On 28 June he was accompanied by Rev. John Elgee to Wexford Bridge where he was hanged along with Beauchamp Bagenal Harvey, John Henry Colclough and Matthew Keugh. They were decapitated, their bodies flung into the River Slaney and their heads were stuck on spikes outside the Courthouse. Later that night some of Grogan's followers dragged the river and retrieved his remains, which were secretly buried in Rathaspeck Church graveyard. Some weeks later his head was also interred at Rathaspeck. All four were shareholders in the same oak bridge that had been completed only three years earlier in 1795. Cornelius Grogan was chairman of the committee behind the construction and he was its main shareholder having donated £1,000.

Following the rebellion, Johnstown estate was seized by the Crown but it was restored to Grogan's brother John in 1810 on payment of a hefty fine. It was John Grogan's son Hamilton who had the present-day Johnstown Castle, with its castellated folly towers, built in the mid-1800s. The family handed the castle and estate to the Irish State in 1945 to serve as an agricultural college and the Irish Agricultural Museum was officially opened in 1979.

Captain Donovan, D-Day and Paddy the Pigeon

The floating 'Mulberry' harbour at 'Gold Beach', Arromanches, Normandy in September 1944. This assured that Allied troops, vehicles and supplies from England could reach France as quickly as possible after D-Day. (Imperial War Museum)

THE DONOVAN family estate and farm at Ballymore near Camolin has been held by the family for 300 years. There have been seven generations of Richard Donovans to own the property since Ballymore House was built by Richard Donovan around 1690. Rickard (1898-1952), was the sixth generation and one of the masterminds behind the planning of D-Day – the Allied landings in Normandy on 6 June 1944.

Aged 9, Rickard was sent to Arnold House preparatory school in London and at the age of 13 he moved to the Royal Naval Colleges on the Isle of Wight and then on to Dartmouth in Devon. At the outbreak of World War I in 1914, he served on *HMS Ocean*, which was part of a massive Allied invasion sent to open up the Dardanelles – the strait that separates European Turkey and Asian Turkey – in 1915. His ship was torpedoed and as the 17-year-old Rickard was last off the ship, the captain sent him back on board to recover the ship's log, lest it fall into Russian hands.

Rickard saw many sea battles throughout World War I. By 1917, he was commanding *Submarine L7* in attacks on Turkish vessels in the Dardanelles at the age of 19, with a crew of teenage naval cadets, some only 15 years of age. While onboard the dangerous and cramped submarines, he contracted tuberculosis which remained untreatable.

Now between the two world wars, Rickard received a military pension in 1927 due to his illness. He had a background in engineering and after the Great War was appointed manager of the submarine construction yard of Beardmore shipbuilders on the Clyde in Scotland. He worked primarily on the development of a cleaner diesel engine for submarines – in order to improve the air quality on board. In 1937 he transferred to the London & Thames Haven Oil Company.

When World War II broke out in 1939, Rickard rejoined the Royal Navy and was assigned to Combined Operations. Following the humiliation of the evacuation of stranded British and other Allied forces in Europe to Britain from Dunkirk in 1940, Lord Louis Mountbatten, Chief of Combined Operations from 1941, focused on the re-invasion of Europe. Rickard Donovan, having risen rapidly through the naval service and noted for being 'an exceptional staff officer in every way', was promoted to the rank of Captain and Assistant Director of Plans. With a small group of men, Rickard led the secret day-to-day work of devising plans for Operation Overlord (D-Day) with Mountbatten as chief of the division.

Captain Rickard Donovan C.B.E. from Ballymore, Camolin.

However, Rickard's health was deteriorating due to the tuberculosis that he contracted in his teenage years and in January 1944 he was hospitalized for a time but did not allow his poor health to interfere with his work. Combined Operations was based in Richmond Terrace in London, where Rickard worked throughout most of the war. The building was connected to the Prime Minister Winston Churchill's offices at 10 Downing Street by an underground passage.

A landing project as huge as Operation Overlord could only be undertaken with the assurance that Allied troops, vehicles and supplies could reach land as quickly as possible. The British developed portable harbours called 'Mulberry' harbours so that troops could be landed close to the shallow waters of Normandy's beaches. They were designed by civil engineer Major Allan Beckett but the American side were doubtful that they would work. Rickard Donovan was asked to devise the building of these prefabricated harbours and turn the project into reality. In 1943, with planning of Operation Overlord now at an advanced stage, two Mulberry harbours, one British/Canadian and one American, were completed. They each consisted of 6 miles of flexible steel roadways that floated on concrete pontoons.

On D-Day, 6 June 1944, the first components of the harbours were towed across the English Channel by tugs, travelling at 5mph, to the Normandy coast and were operational within two weeks. The American harbour at Omaha Beach was soon destroyed in a devastating storm on 19 June, the worst to hit Normandy in 40 years, but the other at Arromanches survived. In the ten

'Into the Jaws of Death' — the iconic photograph taken by U.S. chief photographer's mate, Robert Sargent at 7.40am on 6 June 1944, shows American troops wading through waist-deep water towards 'Omaha Beach'.

Taken in the late 1970s at 'Gold Beach', Arromanches, where British troops landed on D-Day. The photo shows remains of the 'Mulberry' harbour — an artificial harbour that was towed across from England in sections. 2.5 million Allied soldiers and half a million vehicles landed here during its 10 months of operation. (photo: Des Kiely)

months after the Normandy landings, 2,500,000 men, 500,000 vehicles and 4,000,000 tonnes of supplies were landed at 'Gold Beach', Arromanches. In the wake of D-Day, fuel pipes were laid across the Channel and within days were supplying the military with 8,000 tons of fuel daily.

However, the intense stress of planning these mammoth operations began to take its toll on Rickard's health and led to him suffering from extremely high blood pressure.

Rickard was retained by the Admiralty after the war to write the official history of the development of Combined Operations. On his retirement from the Royal Navy in 1945, having served in two world wars, he was awarded a CBE – Commander of the Order of the British Empire – from King George VI as well as the Legion of Merit from U.S. President Harry Truman for outstanding services and achievements. It took two years for the Irish media to acknowledge these awards, much to the disappointment of Rickard, who regarded himself foremost as an Irishman.

He had never told his wife Margaret or any members of his family back in Ballymore what his work entailed. She found him very agitated and concerned in the lead-up to D-Day but did not know why. On the morning of the invasion, he woke Margaret and suggested she turn on the radio.

D-Day was the biggest seaborne and airborne invasion ever staged in world history. Over 4,000 Allied troops were killed on the day, about the same number of Germans and more than 3,000 French civilians. But the massive Allied landings on the beaches of Normandy marked the beginning of the end for Hitler's Third Reich.

Ballinesker Beach in the opening scene of the 1997 film 'Saving Private Ryan'. The location was used due to its similarity to Omaha Beach in Normandy.

Rickard's high blood pressure led to his early death in 1952 at the age of 54. He is buried in a solitary grave in a quiet corner of a field on Ballymore Estate on a hill over-looking his great love: the sea.

Ballinesker Beach, Curracloe, today. (photo Des Kiely)

D-DAY GO-AHEAD FROM MAYO
Though Ireland (then officially Éire) remained neutral throughout the war, weather forecasts continued to be supplied to Britain as part of a secret deal in September 1939 between the two governments. The most north-westerly European meteorological station was at Blacksod Point Lighthouse on the Mayo coast, which also housed the coastguard station and post office. Ted Sweeney was the lighthouse keeper and from the 1930s to the mid-1950s, the lighthouse doubled as a meteorological station, measuring rainfall, wind-speed, wind-direction and cloud formations. During the war, as 1944 approached, Ted was requested to give the weather forecast every hour on the hour. His wife Maureen was the assistant postmistress and she passed on readings from the weather station to Ballina, who forwarded them to Dublin, before the information was secretly transmitted to the British by teleprinter in a code devised by the Americans.

The choice of day to launch the D-Day invasion fell on the supreme commander of the Allied Forces in Europe, General Dwight Eisenhower, and Field Marshal Montgomery. (In January 1921, Montgomery had been appointed Brigade Major of the British Army's 17th Infantry Brigade stationed in Cork City towards the end of the Irish War of Independence).

The invasion was planned for Monday, 5 June, but the following two days were also considered as possible dates because a full moon, clear skies, little wind and low tide were expected – all deemed ideal for seaborne and airborne nighttime landings. Otherwise high winds and rough seas could capsize landing craft and sabotage the amphibious assault; wet weather could bog down the army and thick cloud cover could hinder the necessary air support. An accurate weather forecast was vital for D-Day.

On Friday 2 June, separate observations were taken at various locations by Royal Air Force, Royal Navy and U.S. Air Force meteorologists. The Americans were optimistic that a ridge of high pressure would dominate on the original D-Day date of 5 June. But the British were pessimistic about the forecast for suitable conditions on the day. Agreement could not be reached and this caused serious consternation. But it was the keeper at Blacksod, Ted Sweeney, who would save D-Day from potential disaster.

In the early hours of Saturday 3 June, oblivious to how his forecast was to change the course of the Second World War, Ted sent out his hourly local forecast at 2am: 'Force 6 wind and a rapidly falling barometer', indicating a major storm was due and predicted to move rapidly south-eastwards and would possibly reach the English Channel by 5 June. Later that morning at

11am, a call came through from England to his wife Maureen. It was Maureen's 21st birthday and the caller requested a repeat of the last weather observations Ted had sent earlier. Ted came to the phone and repeated the earlier forecast. An hour later, the same person phoned again asking to 'please check and repeat the whole report'. The weather for Monday 5 June in the English Channel was looking bad.

On Sunday, 4 June at 12pm, Ted sent his latest local report that offered hope to Eisenhower and the Allied commanders to launch D-Day on Tuesday, 6 June: rain

Blacksod Point Lighthouse at the southern tip of Mullet Peninsula, Co. Mayo. (photo: Des Kiely)

clearing and visibility on land and sea becoming very clear.

Scottish meteorologist James Stagg, who had been Operation Overlord's chief forecaster, studied the Blacksod reports and advised Eisenhower. In the early hours of 5 June, at Eisenhower's morning briefing, he reluctantly agreed to delay D-Day by twenty-four hours and announced that the invasion would now proceed on the following day, Tuesday 6 June. A loud cheer went up and complete confidence in a successful invasion was restored. This vital decision was to avert a military catastrophe.

German forecasters had also predicted the stormy conditions in the English Channel for 5 June but they expected that the bad weather would continue over the following two days also. Nazi commanders were not privy to the forecasts from Ireland and believed an Allied invasion was therefore not imminent and so many left their coastal defences. German Field Marshal Rommel, who was commander in Normandy at the time, returned home to his wife for her birthday, which fell on 6 June, and was in Germany when he received news that the invasion had begun.

Dwight Eisenhower served as U.S. President from 1953 to 1961. Approximately 70,000 Irishmen joined the British armed forces in the Second World War with many dying on the beaches of Normandy. On a visit to the John Barry Memorial in Wexford in 1962, he laid a wreath for all Wexford seamen who 'gave their lives that we might live'.

PADDY THE PIGEON

Paddy, a putman pigeon, was bred in 1943 in Carnlough, Co. Antrim, by his owner Andrew Hughes and, with several other pigeons, went into training as a racing pigeon. Having first served at RAF Ballykelly in Co. Derry on air-sea rescue missions, he was delivered to RAF Hurn in Hampshire. Thousands of other pigeons were donated by the racing pigeon fraternity for service during World War II.

On 8 June 1944, two days after D-Day, Paddy was among 30 pigeons taken to France by a unit of the First U.S. Army for undercover missions during the Normandy landings. Paddy was released at 8.15am on 12 June, carrying coded information, attached to his leg, on the Allied advance in Normandy – code-named 'U2'.

Paddy is the only recipient in Ireland of the Dickin Medal for bravery.

Despite poor weather conditions and the threat of German falcons, deployed to intercept Paddy and his comrades, he delivered his message to his home loft in Hampshire after flying 230 miles in a record-breaking 4 hours and 50 minutes. This was the fastest time recorded by a message-carrying pigeon during the Normandy landings, with an average speed of 56mph.

On 1 September 1944, Paddy was awarded the Dickin Medal, the animal equivalent of the Victoria Cross 'for the best recorded time with a message from the Normandy Operations, while serving with the RAF in June 1944'. He is the only recipient of the medal in Ireland. After the war, Paddy was returned to his owner in Carnlough, where he died in 1954, aged 11.

The medal was put into auction in 1999 by Whyte's Auctioneers in Dublin and purchased by pigeon fancier and ex-FCA man, Kevin Spring.

In 2010, a feathered fly-past of pigeons formed part of the Paddy Memorial Day event held at Larne Museum and Arts Centre. A children's book, *Paddy the Pigeon* by Gail Seekamp was published in 2003 and members of Larne and District Historical Society erected a plaque at the harbour in Carnlough in 2009 in memory of one of the borough's most unique wartime heroes.

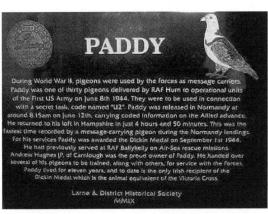

The plaque at the harbour in Carnlough, Co. Antrim, erected in 2009 in memory of the village's wartime hero.

Over 30 years, Kevin covered his entire cottage in seashells

Cliff Cottage or the 'Shell Cottage' above Cullenstown Strand, near Bannow Bay, 1976.

CATHY FFRENCH was a little girl growing up in the 1960s in idyllic Cliff Cottage, located on the cliff road above Cullenstown Strand. The clifftop offers spectacular panoramic views from Kilmore Quay to Hook Head and of Ballyteige Bay and the Saltee and Keeragh Islands. She spent many hours walking on the beach below, collecting seashells, which she would bring home in bags. Cathy would not allow her parents throw them out and her father Kevin was in a quandary — what do with the large collection that was cluttering the house.

Kevin was born in 1921 to Philip and Margaret Ffrench (née Whyte). Margaret, daughter of sea captain George Whyte, was born in Cliff Cottage, which had been in the Whyte family for generations. The original house that stood on the site dated back to 1272, a hundred years after the Anglo-Normans landed in nearby Bannow Bay. The present house dates from about 1700 and the pitch pine roof timbers came from shipwrecks, common along the south coast of County Wexford throughout the centuries.

Kevin Ffrench, who served in the Royal Navy during WWII, decorated his house with seashells between 1970 and 2000.

At the outbreak of WWII in 1939, Kevin enlisted in the Royal Navy as did so many at the time. He was 18 years old and served on *HMS Caradoc*, which was deployed in the Atlantic and assigned to operate off the North American coast. Those were dangerous times and many of his friends who enlisted did not survive the war. Kevin was decorated with three medals on leaving the service in 1942.

In 1945 he married Kathy Keane from Bannow, where they lived for the first eleven years. Cliff Cottage had fallen into disrepair, having been left unoccupied for many years. But they decided to move in and Kevin began to restore the house himself. They had five children and Cathy was the youngest. Kevin was a resourceful man. He kept a 14-foot fishing boat on the beach below the house and would sell mackerel, or whatever his catch was, from the house. He kept cattle and hens and grew vegetables in the adjoining field of rich sandy soil, having added seaweed from the beach to enrich the earth.

It was 1970 and Kevin decided to use some of Cathy's seashell collection to decorate an old flowerpot. He then added shells to the top of the gate piers and front walls of the house. And so began thirty years of painstakingly covering the entire house with seashells; his goal was to leave behind a work of art that would survive long after his death.

Kevin added to the collection that Cathy had begun, sourcing most of the shells from Cullenstown. He collected razor shells from Rosslare Strand, scallops and mussel shells from the fishermen in Kilmore Quay, and oyster and cockle shells from Bannow Bay. He sorted the shells to find exact matches and meticulously measured each one, using his own handmade seven-inch ruler that had the measurements from right to left.

Kevin used sand and cement to apply the shells, and when he had finished

Kevin's handmade ten-inch ruler that he used to match his shells by size.

covering the entire front of the cottage he moved on to the yard and covered all the out-buildings. The cottage is stunningly decorated with over 50,000 seashells. Among the patterns are beautiful inter-pretations of Tuskar Light-house, ships, ships' wheels and sea birds. He also incorporated an old lifebuoy and a porthole from a shipwreck in the designs. Throughout the winter months, Kevin worked out his designs, carefully selecting the correct shells, and applying

Kevin at work on his Tuskar Lighthouse design, late 1980s.

them outside when spring arrived. Also found within Kevin's artwork is the motto of the Royal Marines: *Per Mare Per Terram* (By Sea, By Land). His last work was the pattern of a large dolphin on the gable end of the cottage. The house is one of Ireland's most unique landmarks and is photographed by thousands of visitors every year.

An example of Kevin Ffrench's amazingly symmetrical shellwork.

The oat straw thatch on the roof of the cottage had to be replaced about every ten years and Kevin learned how to maintain it himself. In 1976 it won the Bord Fáilte 'Best Thatched Homestead' award. However, when Hurricane Ophelia struck in October 2017, the worst storm to affect Ireland in 50 years, a large portion of the thatched roof was blown off. Some shell decorations in the courtyard met the same fate. It being a listed building, a partial grant under the Built Heritage Investment Scheme to entirely re-thatch the cottage in oat straw was finally approved in 2019.

In 1914 the Norwegian schooner, *Mexico*, ran aground on the rocks off the Keeragh Islands, within direct sight of Cliff Cottage. The rescue attempt by the Fethard lifeboat resulted in the tragic drowning of nine of its crew, whose bodies were washed up on Cullenstown Strand. One of the *Mexico* crew, a 19-year-old Portuguese sailor, died on

Kevin's interpretation of the ill-fated cargo schooner 'Mexico' that ran aground on the Keeragh Islands, in view of the house, in 1914.

the island from hypothermia. He was later buried at Kilpark in Cullenstown. The neglected cemetery holds the bodies of many unknown seamen who were washed up on Cullenstown Strand in wartime.

George Whyte, Kevin Ffrench's grandfather, supplied blankets and refreshments to some of the crew of the *Mexico* and in appreciation its captain, Ole Edwin Eriksen, presented him with his binoculars, a crosscut saw and a storm lantern from the ship.

Two years before the tragedy on the Keeraghs, the nearby handball alley was built by the local community, including George Whyte. In the 1960s and early '70s it also served as a 'dancehall', and later volleyball, tennis and squash were played. The alley was in danger of being washed away due to severe coastal erosion but has been saved by coastal protection works in recent years.

Captain Ole Edwin Eriksen of the 'Mexico' presented George Whyte with his binoculars and other items in appreciation of the care afforded to him and a number of his crew.

The outer wall of the alley carries a commemorative plaque to four members of the Irish Army Corps of Engineers from the Curragh Camp. They lost their lives in 1941 during WWII at nearby Ballyteigue Burrow, while making safe a sea mine that had been washed ashore. They were named as Sergeant James Curran, Private James Keogh and Private Joseph Tinsley. The fourth soldier, Private Peter Conlon, was badly injured and died some days later. The south

Irish Sea was easily reached by the German submarine fleet from occupied French ports, so the British had closed the sea route to shipping by laying sea mines, but they were prone to break free from their tether and drift ashore, especially after storms.

When Kevin passed away in 2003 at the age of 81, his family erected a plaque on the front of the house that reads: 'Dedicated to the memory of Kevin L. Ffrench who designed and crafted the artistic shellwork on this cottage'. The house continues to be photographed by visitors to Cullenstown, who are in awe of Kevin's wonderful craftsmanship, and photographs of his great artistic work continue to be shared on social media around the world.

Cathy Ffrench outside Cliff Cottage in the 1960s, before her father Kevin began to cover the house with seashells.

Bishopswater Distillery owner shot dead by excise man

The Bishopswater Distillery complex c.1900, on the then unsurfaced road now known as Distillery Road.
(photo: National Library of Ireland)

BISHOPSWATER Distillery operated between 1827 and 1914 on what is now Distillery Road, Wexford. Two of its owners, Nicholas Devereux and Maurice Harvey, were in the company of an excise man on the premises one day in 1830 when the official accidentally shot Harvey through the heart. Bishopswater was probably the only fully-licensed distillery where the owner was shot dead by an excise man, officially known as a 'gauger' – he was the one normally under threat from the distillery!

The 'new line' road, linking Wexford with Duncannon Fort, was constructed by the military in the early 1800s. Two major industries were set up on the route out of Wexford: Bishopswater Distillery in 1827 and the Folly Mill Iron Works (later Pierce's Foundry) in 1847. A consortium of wealthy local businessmen joined forces to establish 'Devereux, Harvey & Co. Distillers'. They included Nicholas Devereux, his father John Devereux, Maurice Harvey and Patrick Breen. John Devereux had operated a small distillery in the area in the late 1700s and Breen had recently purchased Nicholas Dixon's extensive malting business in Castlebridge (later W. B. Nunn & Company). The distillery complex, regarded as a 'model industrial concern', was constructed on a site of some seven acres at a cost of £30,000 (approx. €2.7m in today's terms).

The facility comprised a granary, malting section and a bonded warehouse and had the most modern equipment installed.

The Devereux family were prominent merchants in 19th century Wexford. Richard and John Devereux, brothers of Nicholas, were the owners of over 60 merchant ships – the largest shipping fleet in Ireland. Richard was also a philanthropist who contributed to the construction of schools and churches as well as a convent for the Sisters of Mercy at Summerhill. John was an MP for Wexford Borough in the 1840s and 50s.

Water from the nearby Bishop's Well was used in the distilling process and Bishopswater stream, which ran behind the distillery, provided power to drive the enormous waterwheel. Its waters were said to possess 'various occult properties derived from the blessings of the sainted Bishop of Ferns.' Power was provided by steam and oil at a later date.

Until very recently, every Irish distillery had a permanent customs-and-excise representative present on site. Commonly known as 'gaugers', because their principal task was to gauge the amount and value of spirits produced, they were charged with ensuring government taxation was adhered to. Until 1831, the term 'gauger' was an official one and it was not uncommon for officers to accept bribes and turn a blind eye to any illegal activity in the distillery. Sometimes gaugers were kidnapped or even killed in order to prevent them testifying in court cases against illicit distillers. Once arguably the most important person in a distillery, every distillery was obliged to provide accommodation for a resident excise officer.

Bishopswater Distillery's resident excise officer was John Donald, who was

in the habit of carrying a loaded shotgun. Only three years in business, Nicholas Devereux was conversing with Maurice Harvey and Mr. Donald in the yard of the premises one day in 1830. Birds were regular visitors, attracted by the ready supply of grain. On spotting one passing overhead, John Donald raised his gun and accidentally shot Maurice Harvey, standing about four yards away, through the heart.

The incident made national news at the time. 'Mr. Devereux never heard him speak more,' wrote the *Wexford Herald* reporting on the inquest held later by two local magistrates, L. E. White and G. A. Walker, in front of a jury. 'Did Mr. Donald appear embarrassed after?' a witness was asked. Under the headline: 'Melancholy Death of Maurice Crosbie Harvey, of Wexford, Esq,' the paper stated that the jury returned a verdict of accidental death and John Donald was acquitted. The article ended: 'Mr. Donald, we understand, labours under the greatest agony of mind since the melancholy occurrence.'

By 1833, just six years after opening, the distillery was producing about 200,000 gallons of triple-distilled 'pure pot still whiskey' per annum and was renowned for its great quality. It was sold locally as well as in surrounding counties and a separate warehouse was constructed on Crescent Quay to facilitate exports to Liverpool, Bristol and London. At the time, pot still whiskey was the most popular type in the world. A mix of malted and unmalted barley and unmalted raw barley was distilled in their three pot stills. Sometimes small amounts of raw oats or wheat were added.

Barley was delivered by local farmers to large stores on the quays, where it was dried in adjoining kilns, before being taken by cart to the distillery. There were three old pot stills on site and one of the spirit stores was located underground, cut out of limestone; it was said to have been 'as dry as bone.' There were nine warehouses with a total capacity of 5,000 casks. Unique to Bishopswater was its 20-foot-high 'worm tub'. It contained a coiled pipe called a 'worm' through which cold water travelled and this was used for cooling and condensing alcohol vapours. A stone staircase led to the top of the tank, from which point the harbour and shipping fleet could be observed.

From around the mid-1830s, Nicholas Devereux took full control of the distillery. However, in 1838 the Temperance movement began with the establishment of the Teetotal Abstinence Society, dedicated to lowering consumption of alcohol. Some religious leaders publicly dumped stocks of whiskey and this all had the effect of causing a 35% drop in production at Bishopswater between 1846 and 1866.

Nicholas died in 1840 and was succeeded by his son Richard. His daughter Mary married John Locke, son of the founder of Locke's Distillery, and she herself became active in the distillery in Kilbeggan, Co. Westmeath. On the death of her husband in 1868, she took over the running of the business. In 1847, at the height of the Famine, production ceased temporarily, Richard Devereux believing that grain should be used for food rather than distilling.

The distillery had a visit from British journalist, Alfred Barnard in 1886. He was secretary of *Harper's Weekly Gazette* and visited every working whiskey distillery in Britain and Ireland from 1885 to 1887. The result was the publication of the 500-page *The Whisky Distilleries of the United Kingdom*. Barnard noted that output at Bishopswater had fallen to just 110,000 gallons per annum, amongst the lowest outputs of any distillery operating in Ireland at the time and far below the potential output of 250,000 gallons.

By the early 1900s, the distillery found itself too small to compete with the bigger distilleries in the country and with the rise in the popularity of blended whiskies – as opposed to pot-still whiskey – the distillery was put up for sale in 1909. But it failed to attract a buyer and ceased operation in 1914, after 90 years.

The complex was located across the road from the colossal Pierce's Foundry, which eventually acquired the site and established a bicycle factory there for about ten years, but it did not have great success. Michael Collins was presented with a Pierce double-barred bicycle; the heavy-duty bicycles were marketed as 'service cycles' and Collins wanted the army to be supplied with bicycles made by Pierce rather than by English manufacturers. A number of Pierce's bicycles are on display in the Irish Agriculture Museum at Johnstown Castle. Known as Pierce Bicycle Works and Plough Foundry, they filled the 'worm tub' with rubbish from the works. The main distillery buildings were demolished in the 1940s and 50s and Pierce built housing for the foundry's middle management on the street front on Distillery Road, known as Alvina Brook. The entrance gate to the old distillery remains, bearing the name 'Casa Rio' *(river house)*. The distillery offices are now a private dwelling known as 'Distillery House'.

Bishopswater was not the only distillery operating in the county in this period. Andrew Jameson, a son of the famous John Jameson, set up his own whiskey still on the River Urrin, a tributary of the Slaney, at Fairfield outside Enniscorthy in 1818, in an area still known as The Still. He converted an old forge that produced sword blades into a distillery, which continued to produce whiskey until 1837. Andrew and his second wife Margaret Millar acquired nearby Daphne Castle and had five daughters, all born at Daphne, and their youngest, Annie, was born in 1840. Annie Jameson travelled to Italy to study opera and there met and married Giuseppe Marconi, an Italian aristocrat. They settled near Bologna and had two sons, Alfonso and Guglielmo, who was born in 1874. Guglielmo Marconi, regarded as the 'father of wireless', is known for his pioneering work on long-distance radio transmission and radio telegraphy.

The reconstructed arched entrance to Pierce Bicycle Works and Plough Foundry, formerly Bishopswater Distillery. The photo dates from the 1920s or 30s. Housing for senior managers at Pierce's Foundry was later built close by and the name 'Casa Rio' placed over the archway.

Bannow: the medieval town lost beneath the sand

All that remains of the once-thriving town of Bannow is the ruin of the 12th century St. Mary's Church, which stood at the highest point of the medieval settlement. (photo courtesy Michael Harpur/eoceanic)

THE IMPORTANT town of Bannow once stood near Bannow Island on the eastern entrance to Bannow Bay. Situated at the southwestern tip of the barony of Bargy, it is believed to have grown and prospered around a castle built by the Anglo-Normans, who first landed at this spot in 1169. But 500 years later the town had been abandoned and it disappeared beneath the sand.

THE NORMANS

Having been expelled by the confederation of Irish forces led by Rory O'Connor, the new High King of Ireland, Diarmait Mac Murchada, was deprived of the Kingdom of Leinster, which he had ruled over since 1126. Diarmait sought the help of Henry II, who was King of England and most of France. Henry agreed to send a force of 'Cambro-Normans' from Wales in what became known as the Norman Invasion of Ireland. Diarmait promised the

Anglo-Norman Earl of Pembroke, Richard de Clare (nicknamed 'Strongbow') his daughter Aoife's hand in marriage as well as the succession to Leinster in exchange for sending an army to Ireland. Mac Murchada also promised land to the Anglo-Norman knights who spearheaded the invasion.

Diarmait returned to Ireland with a small Norman force in 1167. It was two years later on 1 May 1169 that Robert FitzStephen arrived at Bannow Bay with an army of about 400 knights and archers, with Bannow Island the focus of the invasion. On 11 May, Maurice de Prendergast sailed from Milford Haven in Pembrokeshire to Bannow Bay with a force of about 600. After a brief skirmish at Duncormick the joint force soon attacked the Norse-Gaelic town of Wexford in what became known as the Siege of Wexford. After almost two days and without the town's walls being breached, Wexford surrendered and was now under Norman control.

In return for his part in the invasion, the Anglo-Norman knight Hervé de Montmorency was granted the baronies of Bargy and Shelburne by Mac Murchada in 1169. De Montmorency had arrived at Bannow Bay with Robert FitzStephen, who married Eva, the daughter of the Chief of Bannow. She

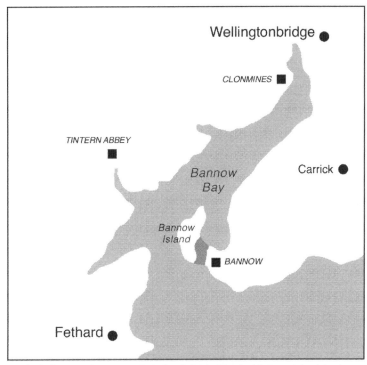

The darkest area is now a sandspit that links the island with the mainland, but in medieval times this was an open channel. © Des Kiely

The medieval parish church of St. Mary's from the southeast corner. (photo: Des Kiely)

had been sent by her father to a convent but escaped to marry FitzStephen. However, they were said to have been later found dead, lying together in snow.

Another knight who landed in the first invasion was Meiler FitzHenry. His son adopted his father's name, and so began the Meyler family name in County Wexford. Colonization under a feudal system soon followed and the building of fortified castles and tower houses commenced.

THE TOWN OF BANNOW

De Montmorency failed in an attempt to found a monastery at Bannow in 1175 but there is strong evidence that he built a fortress and the town of Bannow grew around it during the 13th century. Where he tried in vain to build a monastery in Brendane, the church of St. Brendan was constructed but has since been levelled. St. Mary's Church was built in the late 12th century at the highest point and the centre of the borough of Bannow. The surviving ruins of the church show battlements, which would have given the impression of a defensive structure when viewed from the sea. Up to the mid-1800s, there still existed some remnants of a castle and the once-important town of Bannow but today all that remains is the church ruin.

The church only survived because it was positioned 30 feet above sea level. It consists of a nave and chancel and is surrounded by a graveyard, which is still in use. In 1536, the church was suppressed when Henry VIII was proclaimed head of the Irish Church. A rare elaborate example of a Romanesque font from St. Mary's was brought to the Catholic church in Carrick-on-Bannow.

Bannow Island lies about 200m west of the location of the town of Bannow. Due to shifting sands in Bannow Bay, a sandspit formed that now joins the island with the mainland.

In 1189 De Montmorency became a Benedictine monk at Christ Church Canterbury for a time – the location of the infamous murder of Archbishop Thomas Becket, by knights of King Henry II in 1170. He granted St. Mary's Church and Bannow Island as well as other churches and lands in Bargy to Canterbury before joining the congregation.

An early reference to the town was during the reign of King Edward I (1272-1307). A charter granted New Ross the same privileges as 'those enjoyed by the burgesses of Bannow, Kilkenny and other towns of Leinster'.

Another settlement constructed at the head of Bannow Bay was Clonmines. The Anglo-Norman knight William Marshal founded the town in the early 13th century. But Clonmines too was ultimately abandoned by the late 17th century due to the difficulty in navigating the shallow estuary of mudflats, and so unable to compete with the successful port town of New Ross, which

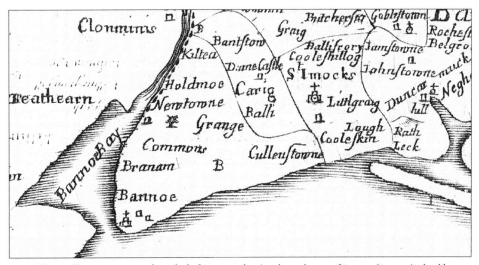

Detail from William Petty's map of Wexford of 1658-59 showing the settlement of Bannoe (Bannow), the old town of Branam (Brandane) and the later abandoned town of Clonminis (Clonmines). Following the Cromwellian Conquest of Ireland in the early 1650s, Petty was appointed to map the forfeited lands, Crown lands and church lands of the country (known as the Down Survey). Petty's Atlas, the first printed atlas of Ireland, was published in 1685.

The town of Clonmines at the head of Bannow Bay was also abandoned after about 400 years.
In the foreground the remains of the Augustinian Priory, founded in 1307, can be seen. The tower house on the right
is known as the 'Black Castle' and the ruined parish church of St. Nicholas stands behind trees on the left.
(photo: Des Kiely)

Marshal had also founded.

The once-thriving town of Bannow, overlooking the entrance to Bannow Bay, prospered over at least 300 years, but gradual silting up of the channel between Bannow and Bannow Island meant boats were no longer able to reach the harbour, and so began the decline of the town. By the mid-1600s, only a dozen or so houses remained. Abandoned houses of timber and clay fell into ruin and in time these ruins were covered by sand. The stones of other buildings were probably removed and used elsewhere. Bannow became known as the *Buried City of Bannow* or the *Irish Herculaneum*.

The National Library of Ireland holds a document, *The Cromwellian Survey of the towns of Wexford, Fethard and Bannow giving the valuation and proprietors in 1641*. The town was laid out in streets with small plots of land between the houses. The survey lists the following streets: High Street, Little Street, Weaver Street, Lady Street, Lackey Street, St Mary's Street, St George's Street, Upper Street, Ivory's Street, Toolock's Street, Back Street, Market Place, St John's Gate, Bride Street, Selskar Street and Hayes Lane.

Although the town no longer existed, Bannow still continued to send two representatives to the Irish Parliament until the Act of Union in 1800. When it was disenfranchised, Charles Loftus, the Marquess of Ely, and Charles Tottenham of Ballycurry, Co. Wicklow, were awarded £15,000 each.

In an 1833 issue of the *Dublin Penny Journal*, Rev. Robert Walsh refers to a 'square mass of solid masonry, about seven feet high' as all that remained of 'the chimney of the town-house peeping above the soil, while the rest of the

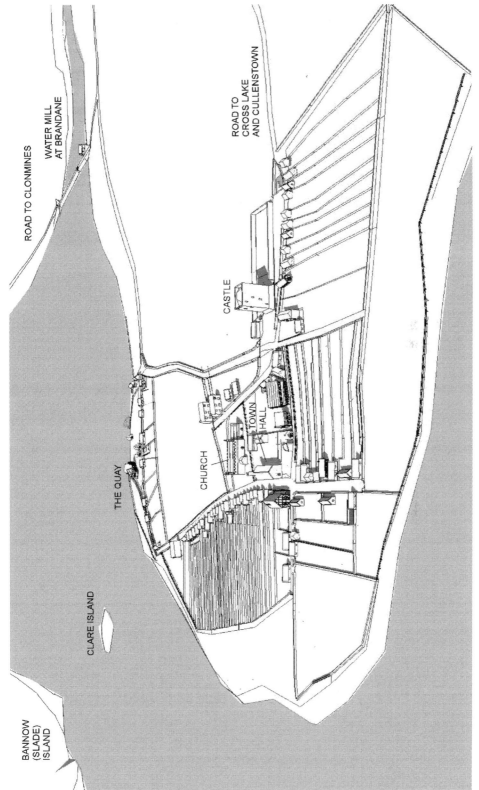

ROAD TO CLONMINES

WATER MILL AT BRANDANE

BANNOW (SLADE) ISLAND

CLARE ISLAND

THE QUAY

CHURCH

TOWN HALL

CASTLE

ROAD TO CROSS LAKE AND CULLENSTOWN

Conjectural image of Bannow around the 1300s from documentary sources. © *Ian Magahy*

Lying in the southeast corner of the nave of St. Mary's Church is this medieval effigy tomb dating from the late 13th century. The inscription in Latin, now illegible, reads 'Here lie John Colfer and Anna Siggin. Pray for them'. Adjacent to it is a sarcophagus or stone coffin and lid. (photos: Des Kiely)

edifice was buried beneath it'. Reference is also made of 'several wide streets, crossing one another … one of them ran down to the mouth of the harbour'. There he found 'a fine quay at the edge of the water two hundred yards in length and higher up the foundation of a very extensive edifice evidently some public building'. In a later issue of the *Penny Journal* in 1850, the same chimney is described as being the remains of the town hall and was being used to post election notices.

The most prominent local landlords in Bannow from the late 17th century were the Boyse family, who lived at Bannow House. The bard and poet Thomas Moore, whose mother Anastasia Codd hailed from Cornmarket in Wexford town, came to Wexford in 1835. He visited his mother's home place as well as his friend and admirer Thomas Boyse. Moore had been to Trinity College with Boyse and the poet was accorded one of the most colourful and unusual welcomes. When he reached Kiltra Bridge near Bannow House, he transferred from his own coach to an open carriage, decorated with laurel branches and flowers. The carriage was drawn by two rows of young men and Boyse rode alongside to the cheers and shouts of a huge crowd. On the front lawn of the new Bannow House, which was still under construction, a large marquee had been erected for dancing and a hot-air balloon swayed overhead. Triumphal banners welcomed Ireland's favourite bard to Bannow. Speeches were made and Moore, greeted with loud hurrahs, praised the 'comfortable and happy appearance of the Boyse demesne' and said he was 'over-whelmed by the kindness of the people's welcome' and reminded the crowd that Wexford was the birthplace of his mother, the daughter of 'honest Tom Codd of the Cornmarket'.

In 1865, some superficial excavations were made at Bannow by Captain Boyse, who discovered the foundations of a large house and a slab bearing the date '1398'. The last member of the Boyse family left the area in 1948.

One notable headstone near the church door records the death of Walter French of Grange, who died in 1701. His age at death is given as 140. He was said to have been travelling from Wexford to his farm in Grange by cart and transporting a load of iron. When his cart broke down, he carried the metal on his back for the rest of the journey but died from exhaustion. Locals said that had he not died on that day, he would have lived on for many more years.

The family vault of the Neale family, owners of the Saltee Islands, lies next to the church ruins. Among those buried here are Prince Michael the First of the Saltees and his wife Princess Anne.

The family vault of the Neale family, owners of the Saltee Islands, stands next to the ruins of St. Mary's Church. (photo: Des Kiely)

Last two Wexfordmen who were hanged for brutal murders

Mountjoy Jail, Dublin, where the remains of twenty-eight men and one woman who were executed in the prison's hanging chamber are buried.

Between 1923 and 1954, thirty people were hanged in the State for murder. The executions were all carried out in Mountjoy Prison in Dublin, two of those who went to the gallows were from County Wexford, and both were executed by the same hangman. The victims of the two murders were men living alone and both were beaten to death for their life savings.

JAMES McHUGH, NEW ROSS

Hanged on 24 November 1926

The first census of the population of the Irish Free State was taken on 18 April 1926. On the evening of 24 April a garda called to the houses in Barrack Lane, a quiet street in New Ross, to collect completed census forms. On calling to the home of pensioner William Dollison, the garda got no reply to his knocks on the door. He saw it was on the latch and so let himself in and made his way to the kitchen, where he made a shocking discovery. He found the body of the 75-year-old man on the floor, lying in a pool of blood, having been beaten to death. The walls were spattered with blood and a blood-stained shoemaker's iron lay under the staircase.

Julia O'Neill, who lived next door, was a 32-year-old widow, a mother of five young children and was eight months pregnant. Her husband had died two years previously from wounds that he suffered while serving in the First World War. It was known around town that Julia was seeing 32-year-old James McHugh from nearby Windmill Lane.

James was a farm labourer but was regularly without employment. Julia had a small war widow's pension and it was believed that she supported him out of this. They were 'living in sin', to use the expression of the time, and he was the father of her unborn child. Their relationship was condemned by the local priest as well as by many in the community, including William Dollison. A group of boys regularly hung around outside Julia's front door and both she and James were convinced that William was behind this intimidation.

William returned to New Ross four years earlier, having lived for 25 years in Liverpool. He had also lived in Dublin and Wexford and was a shoemaker by trade. To supplement his old-age pension he carried out some shoe repair work in the house.

Later on the evening when William's body was discovered, James McHugh was arrested as he walked towards Julia's house. He denied any knowledge of the killing and refused to sign a statement. Julia and her 12-year-old daughter Annie were questioned by the gardaí and gave their version of the events of the night of 23 April. Julia said that James was in her house that evening and they were complaining about William Dollison who they said had encouraged the youngsters to congregate outside her front door. 'Someone should kill that old fellow, Dollison', she claimed James had said and Annie said she heard James saying that he believed William had money in his house.

Eventually, after much deliberation, James and Julia both went next door at about 12.40am to confront their neighbour as he sat by the fire. 'Where's the money?' asked James. When William replied that he had none, James beat him several times over the head with a shoemaker's iron. The attack was heard by their daughter Annie, who was standing outside the house. While Julia began mopping up the blood on the floor, James went upstairs, where he found the elderly man's money. Julia and Annie returned home and James headed down the lane to his own house.

James and Julia were taken into custody and brought to Mountjoy Jail. Julia gave birth to a baby girl on 23 May while in the prison as they awaited trial. The trial, lasting less than five hours, took place in Green Street Courthouse on 27 October. (The courthouse housed the Central Criminal Court, where murders and other serious crimes were tried until 2010, when the new Criminal Courts of Justice building opened). All death sentences were handed down in Green Street.

Before the trial started, Julia pleaded guilty to 'harbouring and maintaining James McHugh, knowing that he had murdered William Dobbison'. She was sentenced to three years' penal servitude.

The main witnesses at James' trial were Julia and her daughter Annie. There was some discussion about allowing testimony from one who had a child by the main witness and from a 12-year-old. But when Annie told the court that she was learning the catechism in school and knew right from wrong, the judge allowed her to give evidence.

When the trial concluded, the judge referred to the relationship between James McHugh and Julia O'Neill in his summing up to the jury. 'You may view these relations,' he said, 'with great disapprobation, but I would ask you to free your minds from any such disapprobation when considering the facts of this case and let your decision be in no way influenced by any displeasure which may have been caused in your minds by the relationship existing between these two people.'

The jury returned a verdict of wilful murder and a sentence of death by hanging was imposed by the judge.

McHugh appealed the sentence. His legal counsel also appealed on his behalf on the grounds that he was 'under the influence of the woman, then in a state of aberration due to her pregnancy'. A petition was signed by about a hundred residents of New Ross, stating that James was of good character and must have been under Julia's influence. It was signed by local clergy, doctors, traders, solicitors and members of the town council and submitted to the Governor General.

Both appeals were rejected, however, and James McHugh was hanged in Mountjoy Jail on 24 November 1926, just seven months after the murder of the New Ross shoemaker.

A garda points to where the body of James Redmond was found close to his caravan at Taghmon in January 1937.

JOHN HORNICK, KILGARVAN, TAGHMON
Hanged on 17 June 1937

The Hornicks were a German Palatinate family who came to County Wexford in the early 1700s. The Palatines were Protestants forced out of their homeland, the Rhineland-Palatine (Pfalz) region of modern-day Germany, by Catholic French troops. Many settled in the Old Ross area.

John Hornick was born in Davidstown in 1893. He worked on the family farm and in 1929 inherited an uncle's farm in Kilgarvan, about two miles from Taghmon. In 1933, John married Rebecca Burren, a farmer's daughter with a £400 dowry from Whitechurch, just north of Campile. They had three children in quick succession and John built a fine new house for his young family on their 45-acre farm in Kilgarvan. He also rented another 20 acres of farmland. John was hard-working, well regarded in the community and had never been in trouble with the law. Now aged 43, he was a regular at local cattle and sheep fairs.

James Redmond, from nearby Tottenham Green, had lived in England and

Canada and returned home to his native County Wexford six years previously with about £200 in savings. He lived in a caravan, which he had parked in a secluded laneway in Taghmon. He survived on unemployment benefit but did a bit of casual work in the locality and, with a small inheritance added, his savings now amounted to over £300. James was a quiet 44-year-old, who had siblings living in the Wexford area. He was closest to his sister Mary, who visited him a couple of times a week.

On the evening of Friday, 15 January 1937, Mary called to the caravan to see James but found the door locked and his bicycle missing. She called again on the following two evenings but there was no sign of her brother and she thought he must have gone away for a few days. On her return on Monday she decided to have a look around and made a grim discovery in a field a short distance away. There, lying on his back, was James's decomposing body. Mary cycled at speed to her brother Patrick's house and they phoned the gardaí. Over £2 in cash, a watch and a penknife were found in James's pockets and, on forcing open the caravan door, they found it was on the whole undisturbed. But a medical examination of the body the next day showed

How the newly-formed Garda Síochána appeared circa 1923. The Irish Free State (1922-37) launched a recruitment campaign and candidates had to be at least 5 feet 9 inches tall, unmarried and between the ages of 19 and 27.

that he had suffered blows from a blunt instrument. He had a fractured skull, a broken jaw, neck injuries and four broken teeth, and so a murder investigation was immediately opened.

James had not been seen in public since Monday 11 January, a week before his body was discovered. An empty Ulster Bank receipt holder was noticed in the caravan and the gardaí learned that on 12 January someone had attempted to withdraw money in James's name from the Ulster Bank in New Ross. The next day £280 in cash was successfully withdrawn in his name from the Dún Laoghaire branch. A deposit receipt for £318 11s 11d had been presented to the bank. The man who had presented himself was not known in the branch and so the cashier asked him to send a telegram from the nearest post office to the Wexford bank, where they did not have a telephone, asking them to phone the Dún Laoghaire branch. After a few private words with his Wexford colleague, the manager asked the man if he had been away in Canada or Australia. 'Yes, out in Canada', he promptly replied and was duly handed the cash.

The gardaí soon turned their attention to John Hornick, who was brought into Taghmon garda station for questioning. He was asked about his movements on 12 and 13 January. He confirmed that he had attended the fair in New Ross and had travelled into Wexford the next day and taken one train to Bray and a second to Dalkey to visit his brother-in-law. He claimed he returned to Wexford that evening and denied going to Dún Laoghaire and cashing a deposit receipt in the name of James Redmond. After making a statement, Hornick was asked to write the name 'James Redmond' six times. The next day he took part in an identity parade and was picked out by both the cashier from Dún Laoghaire and a railway ticket seller from New Ross station. John was then arrested and, when charged with murder, he replied 'I did not kill him anyhow'.

Further investigations found that Hornick had no bank account and just a few small debts. However a shotgun was found near James Redmond's caravan and the matching barrel, which was bent, was discovered concealed in hay in Hornick's farmyard. James's bicycle was also found hidden on the farm.

John Hornick's trial opened in Green Street on 12 April 1937. Evidence from a number of witnesses was that John Hornick was seen carrying a shotgun in the vicinity of James Redmond's caravan both on 10 and 11

January, the day he was last seen alive, as though stalking the victim. The ticket-seller in New Ross station remembered a man fitting Hornick's description purchasing a return ticket from New Ross to Dublin. A cattle dealer in New Ross said that John Hornick had shown him 'a deposit receipt for over £300'. There was also evidence that over a number of days following the withdrawal of cash from James Redmond's account, Hornick had cleared some small debts and bought 13 sheep, 12 heifers, 6 pigs, a horse and saddle, some farm implements as well as clothes and furniture. A handwriting expert concluded that Hornick's signature 'James Redmond' and that given in the Ulster Bank in Dún Laoghaire were written by the same person. The case depended entirely on circumstantial evidence but was conclusive and a guilty verdict from the jury came after just forty minutes.

When Judge O'Byrne asked the accused if there was any reason why he should not impose the death penalty on him, Hornick replied 'No, sir'.

Hornick appealed the sentence but on 1 June his appeal was declined. A petition, signed by over 3,000 people, including thirty-eight TDs, doctors, solicitors, the Archdeacon of Ferns and other clergy, was also turned down by the Government Executive Council. Hornicks' solicitors, Huggard, Brennan and Godfrey of Rowe Street, Wexford, were informed of the rejection in a letter from the Department of the President. Relatives visited him in Mountjoy Jail on the day before his execution. A notice posted on the door of the inner gates read: 'The sentence of the law passed upon John Hornick,

The old execution chamber or hang house in Mountjoy Jail. (photo: Irish Times)

The hangman Thomas Pierrepoint carried out twenty-five of the twenty-nine hangings in Mountjoy between 1923 and 1954.

found guilty of murder, will be carried into execution at 8am tomorrow'. The subsequent inquest in the prison returned a verdict of 'death by judicial hanging, carried out in the interests of justice'.

EXECUTIONS

All prisoners awaiting hanging were held in the 'condemned cell', which was located close to the execution chamber in Mountjoy Jail. Once word came through that the Government had decided against a reprieve, a date for the hanging was sent to the executioner. The time of execution was always carried out at 8am and normally about three weeks after the trial.

Believing it would be difficult to find an Irishman to take on the job of hangman, all 30 hangings in the State were carried out by the Pierrepoint family from Nottinghamshire. Thomas Pierrepoint carried out the first 26 and his nephew Albert was the hangman for the last four. Thomas Pierrepoint is believed to have carried out 294 hangings in his 39-year career and was paid a fee of £15 per hanging. Albert hanged 435 people (including 202 Nazi war criminals in Germany after the Nuremberg trials).

Thomas Pierrepoint, whose brother Henry was also a hangman, would arrive at Mountjoy on the night before the execution and prepare the correct length of rope to suit the height and weight of the condemned prisoner. He also ensured that the scaffold was working properly. The executed prisoners' remains were buried behind the walls of the prison in unmarked graves.

Annie Walsh from County Limerick, the only woman hanged in Mountjoy during this period, was executed in 1925 for the murder of her husband Ned. The last execution to take place in Ireland was that of Michael Manning, hanged in 1954 for the murder of nurse Catherine Cooper in Limerick. In the aftermath of the execution of Manning, Albert Pierrepoint is reputed to have said 'I love hanging Irishmen. They always go quietly and without trouble. They're Christian men and they believe they're going to a better place.'

The burning of Wexford's 'big houses', 1919-1923

The remaining shell of Castleboro House near Clonroche, the former home of Lord Carew, was destroyed in 1923.

DURING the War of Independence (1919-21) and the Civil War (1922-23), a total of 275 'big houses' were destroyed, including nine in County Wexford. The 'big house' or country mansion of the Anglo-Irish landed class was targeted by IRA factions, who regarded them as symbols of the old order of the Protestant Ascendancy in Ireland since the 17th century.

In reprisal for British burning of Republicans' houses during the War of Independence, the 'big house' was made a target and 76 went up in flames, including two in Newtownbarry (Bunclody) and Courtown. But during the Civil War between pro-Treaty and anti-Treaty groups, 199 'big houses' were gutted by arsonists; seven of those in County Wexford. These acts were also in part against the Free State's political elite, both Protestant and Catholic, in retaliation for the execution of Republicans. These included Jim Parle and Jack Creane from Taghmon and Pat Hogan from Wexford, who were shot by firing squad at the old Wexford Jail on Hill Street in March 1923 for possession of arms at Horetown House. (*See Famous Wexford People in History - 2nd Edition*).

In early July 1921, the first County Wexford residences to fall victim in the War of Independence were Ballyrankin House, near Newtownbarry and Ardamine House, Courtown.

BALLYRANKIN HOUSE

The ancestral seat of the Devereux family, Ballyrankin House, was sold to Walter Skrine in 1912. From *The Irish Times* (9 July 1921): 'a party of armed and masked men forced an entry...after the house and furniture had been sprinkled with petrol, it was set on fire...Mr. and Mrs. Skrine were obliged to walk in their night attire to Newtownbarry, which is four miles distant'. The attack was said to have been in retaliation for the burning down of a house in nearby Cramoge by the Black & Tans. Skrine was awarded compensation and purchased nearby Newlands House, renaming it Ballyrankin House. The well-known novelist and playwright Molly Keane (née Skrine) grew up in the old Ballyrankin House but lived most of her life in Ardmore, Co. Waterford, where she died aged 91 in 1996.

ARDAMINE HOUSE

Just two days before the truce ending the War of Independence was signed on 11 July 1921 and five months before the signing of the Anglo-Irish Treaty,

Ardamine House near Courtown, c.1890, was once the seat of the Richards family.

Ardamine House near Courtown was attacked. It was the residence of Major Arthur Richards, a retired British army officer, who was not at home at the time. The caretaker and his wife were allowed to remove their belongings but were not permitted to touch any of the Major's effects. The house was burned to the ground after the furniture was first sprinkled with petrol. Major Richards was later awarded compensation of £30,000 for the house, £7,500 for the furniture and £150 for expenses. He considered rebuilding but was deterred by the estimated high cost. The remains were eventually demolished and the site is now a caravan campsite: Ardamine Holiday Park. All that endures of the Richards estate is the nearby Church of St. John the Evangelist.

Bellevue House and adjoining chapel at Ballyhoge, c.1912.

BELLEVUE HOUSE

The People newspaper reported in February 1923: '...the beautiful residence of the late Captain Anthony Cliffe, which was situate on the banks of the Slaney, near Macmine, was burned to the ground'. It had been attacked some weeks earlier and two rooms in the house were damaged by fire. But on this occasion about fifteen armed men ordered the caretaker Martin Nolan and his family out of the house before setting it alight. The adjoining domestic chapel was spared and is still in use. Bellevue House in Ballyhogue, near Bree, had been in the possession of Anthony Cliffe and his family who moved to England for safety. The Cliffes were popular landlords who had built the village of Ballyhogue for their estate workers in the 1800s.

Castleboro House, home of the Carew family. (photo: National Gallery of Ireland)

CASTLEBORO HOUSE

Some of the county's landed gentry chose to move to England until the political situation stabilized. The Carew family were at one time the greatest landowners in County Wexford with 17,830 acres. Baron Robert Carew and Lady Julia Carew of Castleboro Demesne, between Clonroche and Rathnure, placed the following notice in *The People* in April 1921: 'Lord and Lady Carew are still in London, where they spent the winter. It is doubtful whether they will spend the summer at Castle Boro this year'. The same edition also carried a front-page notice: 'Highly important and interesting sale of very superior antiques and modern furniture, silver, old engravings, oil paintings, library, grand piano. Also costly bedroom furnishing and other effects'. The house was almost entirely emptied in the five-day long auction that followed.

The destruction of Castleboro, one of the finest residences in Leinster, occurred in February 1923, when armed men took hay from the farmyard, soaked it with paraffin, scattered it throughout the main building and set it alight. The fire raged for several hours and completely destroyed the house.

Castleboro was designed by the renowned architect and landscape designer Daniel Robertson, who was also employed for Johnstown Castle, Wells House, Wilton Castle and Ballinkeele House. Robertson was also responsible for the garden designs of Powerscourt and Killruddery in County Wicklow. Castleboro was famous for its gardens, which included terraces that once descended to an artificial lake formed by the Boro River. A tiered fountain marking the midway point of the terraces now stands in the grounds of Park House, Wexford. The demesne has since been converted to farmland. Lord Carew did not live to see his claim for huge compensation satisfied and died aged 62 two months after the fire. Castleboro House is regarded as 'one of the most magnificent ruins in Ireland.'

The original Artramon House near Castlebridge, home to the Le Hunte family.

ARTRAMON HOUSE

For generations, Artramon (or Ardtramont) near Castlebridge was the residence of the Le Hunte family. The house overlooked the River Slaney and the town of Wexford. Sir George Le Hunte was born here in 1852. He served as President of Dominica (1887-94), Secretary of Barbados (1894-97) and Mauritius (1897), Lieutenant-Governor of British New Guinea (1899-1903), Governor of South Australia, 1903-09 and Governor of Trinidad and Tobago from 1909 to 1916. Artramon was razed to the ground in just a few hours on 19 February 1923. It was unfurnished at the time and Sir George was living in Sussex. He died two years later and the house was rebuilt in the style of the original and completed in 1932. The property, with an 800-acre farm and woodland, was bought by Otto Schulte-Frohlinde, the owner of a stud farm in Germany, in 1964. The estate passed to his daughter Ulrike in 1982 and now operates as a luxury guesthouse and working farm.

The well-preserved ruin of 13th century Artramon Castle lies south of the house towards the river. The Anglo-Norman four-storey tower house was built by the Roche family and was in their possession up to the early 16th century.

The elaborate Coolbawn House, Rathnure, built for absentee landlord Francis Bruen on the occasion of his marriage to Lady Catherine Nugent.

COOLBAWN HOUSE

Within a month of the destruction of Castleboro House, the neighbouring Coolbawn House near Rathnure, was set ablaze. The house was built in the early 1800s for Francis Bruen MP, a descendant of James Bruen, one of Cromwell's army who had settled in Boyle, Co. Roscommon, two centuries earlier. Bruen spent so much on the elaborately ornamented house, which was finished in white granite, that locals gave it the name 'Bruen's Folly'. Francis Bruen of Oakpark, Carlow, was an absentee landlord, unpopular with locals and lived in England. In his absence the estate was run by a ruthless agent named Routledge. If any Catholic was behind in their rent they were evicted and their land given to Protestants. The estate was eventually inherited by Bruen's nephew Henry Bruen, who was an MP for County Carlow, and he later sold it around 1919 to James Dier. The house met the same fate as the others when it was burned to the ground by the IRA in February 1923. The ruin is impressive to visit and the building is still of great architectural interest.

WILTON CASTLE

Before the week was out, the arsonists' next target was Wilton Castle near Bree. Like Coolbawn and Castleboro, it too stood close to the Boro River. In 1695, the original Wilton House was purchased by William Alcock from Captain Thornhill, a Cromwellian soldier, who had been granted the house. Another William Alcock, who was MP for County Waterford, gained notoriety

Wilton Castle near Bree in its former glory. (photo: National Library of Ireland)

in 1807 when he shot dead his election opponent, John Colclough of Tintern Abbey, in a duel near Ferrycarrig. Alcock stood trial for murder but was acquitted. His brother, Harry Alcock, succeeded to the Wilton estate and he employed Daniel Robertson, who also designed Castleboro House, to remodel the castle.

In 1923, the castle was the residence of Captain Philip Alcock, a former High Sheriff of Wexford, who had left for England with his wife and children about a year earlier, fearing it was too dangerous to remain. He had removed the most valuable furniture a number of weeks before his fears were realized. In early March 1923, a raiding party of about thirty armed men arrived and ordered the caretaker James Stynes to hand over the keys. The arsonists broke all the ground-floor windows, sprinkled the floors with petrol and set the house alight.

The land was later sold by the Land Commission to Sean Windsor, a local man who grew up on the adjoining farm. A two-storey wing of the castle has been carefully restored and it now operates as a hotel and wedding venue.

BALLYNASTRAGH HOUSE

The ancestral seat of the Esmonde family was Ballynastragh, near Gorey. Of the thirty-seven houses owned by senators in the newly-formed Irish Free State and burned down in the first quarter of 1923, about twenty were in the possession of old landed families. Senator Sir Thomas Grattan Esmonde was married to Louisa, granddaughter of the famous politician, Henry Grattan. While the senator was in London on business, his brother Colonel Laurence and five servants were the only occupants when about 50 anti-Treaty IRA members arrived on the night of 9 March 1923.

The raiders gave them ten minutes to leave but the Colonel was given permission to remove a golden chalice and sets of vestments from the little chapel in the upper portion of the building. The house was then set alight and the flames could be seen from up to ten miles away. The family art collection had been removed just a few days before the fire. But a very historic archive of the Esmonde family's role in politics from the 16th century was destroyed.

In a statement to the Press Association by Sir Thomas as he left London to return to Dublin, he said: 'I received a wire yesterday that my house had been burned down, and I must say that it came as a surprise to me. The only reason for such an act, so far as I know, is that I am a Senator of the Irish Free State'. He later sought compensation and was eager to rebuild Ballynastragh but discovered that the insurance on the house did not cover damage caused by civil disturbance. He was finally awarded £44,800 by Gorey District Council and built an entirely new but much smaller house in its place.

Ballynastragh House, Gorey, seat of the Esmonde family. (photo: National Library of Ireland)

Upton House, Kilmuckridge, home of the Bryan family, c.1912.
(photo: National Architectural Archive)

UPTON HOUSE

According to Samuel Lewis in his *Topographical Dictionary of Ireland*, 1837, Upton was one of the principal seats in Kilmuckridge and 'the handsome residence of W. Monton, Esq., commanding an extensive view of the sea coast'. The house later passed to Isaac Bryan, the first of the Bryan family to reside at Upton. It was rented out for a number of years and Frederick Hughes and his wife Ann (née Bolton) lived there until 1905, when they moved to Ballycross House, Bridgetown, the family seat of the Rowe family.

On the night of 14 March 1923, Upton House became the last of the 'big houses' in the county to be torched by anti-Treaty republicans and was burned to the ground. The local coastguard station at Morriscastle and the RIC station were also set alight on the same night. Lt-Col. Loftus Anthony Bryan, formerly High Sheriff of Wexford in 1892, was the owner at the time and also the proprietor of Borrmount House, near Enniscorthy. Today there is no trace of Upton and a modern house now stands in its place.

The IRA Chief of Staff, Liam Lynch, had explicitly ordered the burning of the 'big houses' in reprisal for the Free State's execution policy but the attacks were largely violence against property rather than people. When Lynch was shot dead by Free State soldiers in April 1923, this effectively ended the Civil War. The Land Commission Act of 1923 made provision for the compulsory purchase of land owned by non-Irish citizens, allowing for it to be divided out among local families. However, some large estates survived where their owners could show that the land was being actively farmed.

Dunbrody: the castle the Etchinghams never completed

Dunbrody Castle with Dunbrody Abbey in the background. (photo: Des Kiely)

RAYMOND LE GROS led the second Anglo-Norman invasion in 1170, landing at Baginbun. Another knight, Hervé de Montmorency, quickly joined him. Richard de Clare (known as 'Strongbow'), an uncle of De Montmorency, landed later at Passage East.

Lands were soon settled by the Anglo-Norman invaders. De Montmorency was instructed by Richard de Clare, now Lord of Leinster, to have a Cistercian abbey built in County Wexford. St. Mary's Abbey, located near Abbey Street in Dublin, took up the challenge in 1182. Dunbrody Abbey, on the banks of the Pill (or Campile) River, a tributary of the River Suir, was completed sometime around 1220 and the site was named the Port of St. Mary's. Hervé de Montmorency was its first abbot and he died there in 1205, aged 75.

It seems relations with nearby Tintern Abbey were not always harmonious. Another abbot of Dunbrody, William de Ross, along with two monks, Adam and Hugh Barry, were accused of imprisoning a monk from Tintern named Thomas Herlyn and stealing two of his horses. They also expelled the abbot of Tintern, Thomas de Wiggemore, and relieved him of three horses. But the three Dundrody residents were acquitted of all charges.

Three centuries passed before Henry VIII was granted the title 'King of Ireland' and head of the 'Church in Ireland' in 1542. As part of his attempt to establish the state church in the Kingdom of Ireland, abbeys, priories, convents and friaries had been disbanded. The last abbot of Dunbrody, Alexander Devereux, handed over the property in 1536 before it was plundered and made unfit for monks to return. In the south-west of County Wexford the confiscated church lands of Dunbrody, Tintern and Kilcloggan were granted to the Etchingham, Colclough and Loftus families respectively.

Sir Osborne Etchingham came from Suffolk and was a marshal in the King's army in Ireland. He was a member of the Privy Council of Ireland and a high official in the court of Henry VIII. He was also a fourth cousin of Anne Boleyn, who was Queen of England as the second wife of Henry VIII. She was beheaded in 1536, having been accused of adultery.

In 1545, Sir Osborne petitioned for the grant of the ruined Dunbrody Abbey which he received the following year. In the charter from Henry VIII dated 4 October 1546, he 'granted Sir Osborne Itchingham, Knight, and the heirs male of his body, the Monastery of Dunbroady, the Grange of Dunbroady, three fishing weirs, mills, and titles, the customs of the town of Coole, and all the possessions of the dissolved Monastery, in the county of Wexford, to

The southern section of the church at Dunbrody Abbey over which the Etchinghams built their Tudor-style residence, photographed c.1900. (photo: National Library of Ireland)

hold in capite by Knight's service, at a rent of £3 10s 6d.' But he probably never occupied the property because he died in that same year.

In 1565, the Etchinghams built a Tudor-style residence above the southern transept of the church in the abbey. They also occupied castles at Ballyhack and Duncannon.

Sir Osborne Etchingham was succeeded by his son Edward, a wild character by all accounts. He got involved at one stage with pirates and was arrested and held in Duncannon Fort, which stood on his own estate lands. Edward escaped and allegedly died in the Tower of London in 1582. After much dispute, the lands passed to his nephew, Sir John Etchingham, in 1602. Sir John resided in Ballyhack Castle and died there in 1616. The son of Sir John Etchingham – another John – married Sarah Loftus, daughter of Sir Adam Loftus of Kilcloggan, in 1618.

Sir John Etchingham began the construction of Dunbrody Castle, a tower house situated a short distance from and within sight of the abbey. It incorporated parts of a much earlier castle dating back to the 1300s and was to be a large two-storey affair with four round turrets on the corners. A bawn or defensive wall surrounded the castle. But with the onset of the Confederate Rebellion in 1641, the Etchinghams fled Dunbrody.

The Confederate Wars were between the Catholic gentry and clergy on one side and the Protestant and Scottish Presbyterian planters on the other. Following the Rebellion of 1641, the Irish Catholic Confederation was established with Kilkenny its capital. The Confederation ruled over about two-thirds of the country in 1642 as a de facto government while Charles I was king of England, Scotland and Ireland. There were attacks on the Dunbrody lands at Ballyhack Castle and Duncannon Fort while Ramsgrange was burned to the ground. Charles I was executed in London in 1649 and later that year Cromwell arrived in Ireland.

John Etchingham and Sarah Loftus had two sons, Osborne and Adam, who never married, and a daughter, Jane, born in December 1646. Sir John, in his will made in 1650 shortly before his own death, left all his estates to his then 3-year-old daughter Jane. When aged only 13, Jane married Sir Arthur Chichester in March 1660. Sir Arthur served in the Irish House of Commons as MP for Dungannon. He was also made an Irish Privy Counsellor and inherited the title 2nd Marquess of Donegall in 1675, but he died just three years later. Jane's grandson, John Chichester, inherited Dunbrody in 1723.

In the early 1800s, the ground floor of the unfinished Dunbrody Castle was converted into a temporary dwelling and occupied by Lieutenant John Kennedy, who was estate manager for the Chichesters as well as the Colcloughs of nearby Tintern estate.

The lands at King's Bay formed part of the Dunbrody estate, now in the possession of the Chichesters. Dunbrody Park was built in 1819 by Spencer Chichester and completed by Arthur Chichester in 1831. The estate village was named Arthurstown and the pier was constructed in 1829. Dunbrody Park, on over 200 acres, was sold by Patrick Chichester in 1996 but the Chichesters still live on the grounds. It is now known as Dunbrody House, a country house hotel and cookery school run by the well-known chef Kevin Dundon.

In 1911, the Chichester family handed Dunbrody Abbey over to the Board of Works. It opened to the public, after extensive renovations, in 1992. Dunbrody Castle and Abbey lie about 3km from Campile. They are open to visitors from May to September and part of the Etchinghams' unfinished castle has been converted into a craft shop. The castle garden includes an intricate maze made up of 1,500 yew trees, one of only two full-sized mazes in Ireland.

The entrance to the craft shop located in the unfinished Dunbrody Castle. (photo: Des Kiely)

Wexford ship that rescued 168 German sailors in WWII

The MV Kerlogue was attacked by both sides in WWII but also rescued people from the two sides.

29 DECEMBER 1943, a small coaster, the MV *Kerlogue*, was carrying a cargo of oranges from Lisbon to Dublin on behalf of the Wexford Steamship Company. In the Bay of Biscay, it steered towards the survivors of a naval battle. Two Royal Navy cruisers had shelled a flotilla of German ships from a distance, sinking the German destroyer, *Z27*, and its two torpedo escort boats. The sea was strewn with more than 700 men: floating corpses in life jackets, survivors on rafts and others clinging desperately to pieces of wreckage.

The Wexford Steamship Company took delivery of the *Kerlogue* from a Rotterdam shipyard in 1938, a year before the outbreak of WWII. The shallow-hulled ship, 43 metres long, carried a crew of eleven and was intended for trading between ports around the Irish coast. These coasters were suited for shallow waters and unsuited for the oceans.

The outbreak of the war meant that most British and US ships were no longer trading with Ireland. Coasters like the *Kerlogue* were forced to sail to distant ports for which they were not constructed. They travelled unarmed with bright lights and had the tricolour and the word 'EIRE' on their sides and decks, identifying themselves as neutral. However, during WWII about twenty percent of seamen serving on Irish ships perished; the victims of attacks from both the Allied and Axis sides. Of the 800 crew working on Irish ships, 149 men died. Allied shipping could not stop to pick up survivors but Irish vessels answered all distress calls and rescued 534 seamen from both sides of the conflict. On St. Patrick's Day 1940, the Taoiseach, Éamon de Valera complained that 'no country had ever been more effectively blockaded because of the activities of belligerents.'

WILD ROSE RESCUE, 2 APRIL 1941

A British convoy was attacked by the Luftwaffe about two miles south of Tuskar Rock. An oil tanker was left burning and another vessel carrying coal, the Wild Rose, was crippled and sinking. The Kerlogue, under the command of Captain Samuel Owens from Carrickfergus, had left Wexford on a passage to Cardiff and altered course when the distress rockets were spotted. There were no survivors from the oil tanker and the two lifeboats on the Wild Rose could not be launched. The Kerlogue took the crew of thirteen on board and with the Wild Rose in tow, beached it on Rosslare Strand. The salvage case was later heard in Dublin, where Justice Conor Maguire commented that: 'The master of the Kerlogue had shown enterprise and courage on the occasion.' The Kerlogue was awarded £4,000 and the Wild Rose was repaired by the Liffey Dockyard.

RAF ATTACK, 23 OCTOBER 1943

Ireland was a net food exporter, mainly to Britain, from where coal and

The Liverpool-registered Wild Rose was attacked near Tuskar Rock and salvaged by the Kerlogue.

manufactured goods arrived back in this country. Throughout the war, the 'Lisbon run' operated between Ireland and Portugal, bringing back fertilizer and fruits from Spain and Portugal, as well as goods trans-shipped from the Americas, such as wheat from Canada. Irish shipping, for its own safety, agreed to sail west of the 12-degree west longitude line.

On the afternoon of 23 October 1943, sailing from Port Talbot in South Wales to Lisbon with a cargo of coal, the *Kerlogue* was 130 miles south of Ireland when it was circled by a Sunderland flying boat from the Royal Australian Air Force. Three hours later, despite the *Kerlogue* being lit and having an Irish flag and the letters 'EIRE' painted in white on its deck and sides, it was attacked by two RAF Mosquito fighter planes of the 307 Polish Night Fighter Squadron, nicknamed the 'Eagle Owls'. They repeatedly dived on the *Kerlogue*, firing their guns for over twenty minutes. Captain Desmond Fortune, who was in command, suffered fractures to both legs. Chief officer Denis Valencie took command while other crew members sustained shrapnel wounds. The bridge was destroyed as well as the radio transmitter and compass, both lifeboats were crushed and the engine room was flooding.

Ironically, it was the British cargo that the *Kerlogue* was carrying that saved the ship and its crew from catastrophe. The cannon shells that penetrated the deck lodged in the coal and never reached the hull. At six in the evening, another RAAF Sunderland flew overhead. The *Kerlogue's* signal lamp was still working and they requested an escort and medical help. But the Sunderland replied that they were unable to render assistance. The pumps however kept working and managed to keep enough water out as the ship limped slowly into Cork.

The Taoiseach, Éamon de Valera, said in a statement in the Dáil on the 2 December 1943: 'They [the British] informed us that the attacking plane did not identify the ship as Irish and at the time of the attack *Kerlogue* was sailing off course...the British government for that reason will not accept responsibility for the attack but are prepared to make a payment ex-gratia to the injured men.'

The British Naval Attaché in Dublin said it was 'unfortunate from a British point of view...' that Captain Fortune had been involved in the *Kerlogue* incident as he was '...always ready to pass on any information in his possession.' The RAF would not apportion blame on the Poles and although the *Kerlogue* was 'east of 12 degrees west...anyone but Polish pilots would have hesitated to attack.'

Captain Fortune would never walk again unaided. The *Kerlogue* was repaired in Cork and Captain Thomas Donohue, from Dungarvan, now took command. Donohue had been captain of *The Lady Belle* of Waterford which was pounded by the Luftwaffe in the Irish Sea in March 1941. He was also captain of the SS *Irish Oak* in May 1943 when it was torpedoed and sunk by *U-607* in the mid-Atlantic. Together with his crew he spent eight hours in a lifeboat before being rescued.

From records released under the thirty-year rule, the first RAAF Sunderland reported: '12.55, Sighted Eire merchant vessel *Kerlogue* in 50°03' north, 9°16' west.' The two RAF Mosquito planes reported: '16.17, 48°55' north, 9°13' west. Sighted and attacked with cannon 1,500 ton merchant vessel flying French flag and word EMPO clearly discerned on starboard side – the word France also on her bows. The vessel, which returned fire with cannon without effect, was left circling with smoke issuing from it...' (The *Kerlogue* was clearly marked, 335 tons and unarmed). The report from the second RAAF Sunderland read: '18.05, Eire merchant vessel *Kerlogue* sighted in 49°49' north 9°11' west.'

Some of the Kerlogue crew: Tom Grannell, Tom O'Neill, Richard Roche, Gary Roche and John 'Chum' Roche. (courtesy Maritime Institute of Ireland)

GERMAN RESCUE, 29 DECEMBER 1943

The *Kerlogue* left Lisbon on Christmas Day 1943 on a routine passage to Dublin through the Bay of Biscay with a cargo of oranges from Lisbon. A German warplane repeatedly circled overhead, flashing the signal 'follow me' to alert it to carnage nearby. They altered their course to offer assistance. Chief officer Denis Valencie later recalled in Captain Frank Forde's book *The Long Watch*: 'As rafts rose into view on the crests of the giant waves, we could see men on them and others clinging to their sides. At first we did not know whether they were Allies or Axis until somebody noticed the long ribbons trailing downward from behind a seaman's cap, which denoted they were German navy men.'

A large German destroyer, Z27, and its two escort boats were sunk in the battle with the Royal Navy. The little coaster bravely approached through the enormous waves and began to pluck survivors from the swelling sea. The crew of the *Kerlogue* spent ten hours hauling young men, many clinging to pieces of debris, onto its deck. They managed to squeeze 168 on board but Captain Donohue had to give the order to leave the rest to their fate. There was no doctor and the ship's medical supplies were totally inadequate but the crew treated the injured as best as they could and supplied them with lots of hot orange juice. From *The Long Watch*: 'cabins, storerooms, and alleyways were soon packed with shivering, soaked and sodden men; others were placed in the engine room where it became so crowded that chief engineer Eric Giggins could not move around to attend his machinery, and so by signs – as none spoke English – he got the survivors to operate the instruments he could not reach.' Fourteen more were packed into the wheelhouse, leaving the helmsman, Tom Grannell of Wexford, barely room to steer the ship.

The highest ranking German rescued was Lt.-Commander Joachim Quedenfeld. He requested Donohue to land his men at La Rochelle or Brest in German-controlled France but Donohue refused. He also ignored British demands to land at Fishguard and headed for Cork, the nearest port. They arrived over two days later at 2am on New Year's Day 1944, escorted by a tender with medical personnel on board, to Cobh quay. Three of the rescued Germans had died en route to Cork and were buried at sea, and a fourth succumbed to his burns after reaching Cork. The wounded were taken to local hospitals and all 164 were eventually moved to the Curragh Internment Camp, where they remained until the end of the war. The *Kerlogue* finally made it back to Dublin on 5 January.

The German ambassador, Dr. Eduard Hempel, wrote to Captain Donohue: '...to you and your crew my profound gratitude as well as my high appreciation of unhesitating valiant spirit which has prompted you to perform the exemplary deed, worthy of the great tradition of Irish gallantry and humanity.'

In 1994, fifty years later, six German naval ships visited Dún Laoghaire. A ceremony in the Old Mariners' Church was attended by President Mary Robinson. Some of the German survivors presented the crew members of the *Kerlogue*, among them Tom O'Neill and Richard Roche from Wexford, with a set of sketches of the rescue, drawn by one of the rescued seamen, Hans Helmut Karsch, while he was interned in the Curragh.

One of the crew was Wexfordman Gary Roche, third engineer and the father of former Government minister Dick Roche. 'My father didn't speak about it an awful lot...the thing that haunted him was the men they had to leave in the water,' said Dick. 'He very graphically described all the men, who were barely hanging onto life at that stage, and calling "comrade, comrade". I know that image stayed with him through his life.'

The brave crew risked their lives to save the drowning Germans, whom they saw not as combatants but as fellow sailors. The story of the rescue was recreated in the 2016 novel *The Lonely Sea and Sky* by Dermot Bolger. His father sailed on board the *Kerlogue*'s sister ship, the MV *Edenvale* during the war. The *Kerlogue* was sold to Norway in 1957 and renamed *Munken*. It sank off Lindesnes in 1960.

A memorial to the crew of the Kerlogue was erected on Wexford Quay in 2015. (photo: Des Kiely)

'I was a slave labourer in the House of Mercy'

A Magdalene laundry similar to the 'House of Mercy for Poor Servants' at Summerhill in Wexford.

PEGGY CULLEN was born in Ballywilliam, between New Ross and Rathnure, in 1940. She was the youngest of four and her father worked as a farm manager for a meagre wage, with the family permitted to live in a small house on the farm. On leaving primary school in nearby Templeludigan at the age of 12, her mother was concerned about her approaching teenage years and they also could not afford to pay for her education. The parish priest in Templeludigan, Fr. Clancy, suggested that Peggy should go to the Sisters of Mercy in Wexford, where she would receive free education and board. Peggy was excited at the prospect and hoped this would help her fulfil her ambition to be a nurse. This is her story as told to me.

In September 1953, two months before her thirteenth birthday, her father took her on his pony and trap and put her on a train to Wexford. She travelled alone and found her way to the Sisters of Mercy convent in Summerhill. There she was received by a reverend mother, who brought her straight to the laundry where she was to spend the next four years as inmate no. 73.

Between 1953 and 1957, Peggy received no education whatsoever and had no access to books, newspapers or even paper. The Sisters of Mercy ran an orphanage on the site and next to this was what they called a 'training centre'. But Summerhill Training Centre was run as a Magdalene laundry. Sr. Mary of the Sacred Heart was in charge of the facility. Between 20-25 girls worked six days a week there as child labourers – laundering clothes for local hotels such as the Talbot, White's and the County Hotel as well as Johnstown Castle (then a residential horticultural college) and private houses. The 'Sisters of Mercy Laundry' operated in direct competition with the local family-owned Celtic Laundry (now Celtic Linen).

A typical day for the girls began with Mass at 6am, breakfast, consisting of tea and bread, at 7am followed by scrubbing and polishing the dormitory floors and long corridors. After washing up from breakfast, work in the laundry began at 8.30am and ended at 9pm. But the girls often worked up to midnight and the nuns would dim the lights after 9pm in order not to alert St. Peter's Seminary next door that the inmates were still working. Sunday was the only day that the laundry did not operate but the girls still had to clean and polish the dormitories.

Every Friday the laundry van, a green Ford with 'Sisters of Mercy Laundry' on the side, entered through the gate of the convent to collect the week's laundry. The driver, who lived in the gatehouse, was joined by a trusted helper who later joined the community. She assisted in delivering the laundry and collecting payment for the nuns, but the girls received not a penny for their work.

The Sisters of Mercy convent in Summerhill, Wexford. It was demolished in the 1990s.

Peggy claims that the girls in the laundry had no visitors for the four years she was there. They had no contact with the girls in the orphanage next door, who believed the laundry inmates were penitents and so they would run away when they encountered them. Speaking was forbidden and the girls' birthdays were never acknowledged. Peggy says the children lived in fear and walked with their heads bowed. Once a year, dressed in blue cloaks and veils as 'Children of Mary', the girls paraded through the streets of the town to the grotto at Rocklands. They were warned that if they attempted to escape that the gardaí would catch them and take them back to the convent.

Inmate no. 83 was Breda Croghan, who now lives in Dublin. Breda was born in the Old County Home in Enniscorthy after her unmarried mother became pregnant. Aged two-and-a-half, she was put into St. Aidan's Orphanage in Enniscorthy before being sent to live with foster parents near Kiltealy. When she was seven years old, Breda was driven to Summerhill by a priest and was immediately given the laundry uniform. After two years working there, she managed to escape in the laundry van, hiding under the laundry baskets, but was caught and returned by the gardaí. A year later she escaped again and this time made it as far as Dublin. 'The biggest sin of all was wetting the bed. There would be a bed inspection in the mornings and if the nuns found wet sheets they would strip them off the beds and tie them around the girls' faces. They'd do the same if there was blood on the bed when you had your period,' said Breda.

Peggy tells the story of when her first period came on. 'I didn't know what it was; I thought I was bleeding to death', she says, 'and I thought they'll surely send me home now. They could abuse me all they wanted but I wasn't going to leave the bed.' The following day a doctor was called. 'I was put in a real posh bed with white sheets' and when the doctor arrived he explained: 'You won't have problems when you get married and you'll be fine,' and Peggy was returned straight away to work in the laundry.

Some of the older girls were contracted out to work as domestic servants. When Peggy was 17, she was sent to a family in Newtown but she left after a short time. She took a train to Rathgaroge and walked the two miles to her home in Ballywilliam. But Peggy did not get a warm welcome after four years. 'You'll have to get a job quickly because you can't stay here,' said her mother. Failing to find a job after six months, she headed for London with very basic education and a poor grasp of the English language. It was then that she realized the full extent of the damage done to her at Summerhill. 'My English was dreadful and I had no maths,' she explains. In May 1958, Peggy enrolled as a trainee nurse at St. Benedict's Hospital and also studied at Purley Hospital, where she received free tutoring in English and mathematics in the evenings in order to help her write patients' daily reports.

While in London, Peggy met and fell in love with William Cowman, a County Waterford native from Dunhill, near Annestown. They married in 1962 and had two children but William died aged only 49 in 1989.

Peggy Cullen, aged 19, having been awarded 'Best Practical Nurse' at St. Benedict's Hospital in London.

MAGDALENE LAUNDRIES

The first Magdalene institution, the 'Magdalen Hospital for the Reception of Penitent Prostitutes', was founded in London in 1758. The first asylum or laundry in Ireland was the 'Magdalene Asylum for Penitent Females', which opened in 1767 on Leeson Street, Dublin. The last Magdalene laundry in Ireland closed in 1996.

The largest Irish Magdalene laundry was at High Park, Drumcondra, Dublin and was run by the Sisters of Our Lady of Charity of Refuge. When a business they had invested in went bust, they were forced to sell some of their land

Peggy and her fiancé William Cowman, a County Waterford native, pictured in London.

holdings to cover their losses. In 1993 they sold a tract of land to developers for £1.5m. Seven years later in 2000, the old laundry building was sold for €6.68m and in 2006, at the height of the 'Celtic Tiger', they sold a green area of 6.7 acres inside the compound for over €63m. However, when construction workers moved into the land that they bought in 1993, they were shocked to find an unmarked communal burial pit containing the remains of 133 females. The Department of the Environment ordered undertakers to exhume the bodies. Despite being told that there were no more, the undertakers continued to dig deeper and found a further 22. The nuns agreed to split the cost of removal and cremation of the remains and burial of their ashes in another mass grave in Glasnevin Cemetery. Of the 155 corpses that were found, only 75 death certificates existed.

The discovery of the High Park mass grave led to articles in the media about the religious institutions and also inspired the song *The Magdalene Laundries* written by Canadian singer-songwriter Joni Mitchell. A government inquiry was called for by the UN Committee on the Rights of the Child. The courts had regularly sent girls convicted of petty crimes to the laundries and the gardaí returned those who managed to escape. Contracts were awarded to the laundries by State Bodies and yet the government resisted the call for compensation to survivors.

In 2011, the United Nations Committee Against Torture urged Ireland to investigate allegations against the laundries. This resulted in the McAleese Report, which was published in 2013 and was critical of the religious orders, who denied the girls an education and contact with the outside world. It also concluded that there was 'significant State collusion in the admission of

The Sisters of Mercy convent complex at Summerhill.

thousands of women into the institutions.' Although an immediate apology was not forthcoming from the State, the Taoiseach Enda Kenny apologized in the Dáil two weeks later to the women for the hurt they endured in the laundries, saying: 'This is a national shame for which I'm deeply sorry and offer my full apologies.'

But just two days after the release of the report, a pair of nuns agreed to be interviewed anonymously on RTE Radio 1. When asked to apologize they responded: 'Apologize for what? Apologize for providing a service? We provided a free service for the country.' The response from the Catholic League in the U.S. was: 'No one was imprisoned, nor forced against her will to stay. There was no slave labour... It's all a lie.'

The Magdalen Restorative Justice Scheme was established following the McAleese Report for the benefit of women who were admitted to and worked in Ireland's 10 Magdalen institutions as well as St. Mary's 'Training Centre', Stanhope Street in Dublin and the Sisters of Mercy 'Training Centre' in Wexford, collectively called the 'Magdalen institutions'. By late 2018, the scheme had paid out €33m to almost 700 women, who worked and resided in the 12 institutions.

The religious congregations, including the Sisters of Mercy, have refused government demands to contribute to the compensation fund for surviving victims. The Sisters of Mercy claim that 'young girls of good character were trained in domestic work' and that the laundry was opened 'to provide means for their support.' Breda Croghan's response was: 'if they are saying that this didn't happen well I must be living in a dream, because I remember it all... the cruelty and the physical abuse we suffered there.'

Peggy Cowman (née Cullen) returned to New Ross after 50 years in London. (photo: Des Kiely)

Peggy returned to Ireland after 50 years in London and now lives in New Ross. She says many people still don't believe her story. She is not looking for money but simply wants the truth to be told and for her to be believed.

Edwardian playboy was first to fly from Britain to Ireland

Denys Corbett-Wilson at Fishguard just before his departure at 5.47am on 22 April 1912.

EXACTLY one week after the *Titanic* sank in the North Atlantic, 30-year-old Denys Corbett-Wilson took off from Fishguard on 22 April 1912 and crash-landed near Enniscorthy 100 minutes later. He was the first person to make the crossing between Britain and Ireland, seven years before the first non-stop transatlantic flight from Canada to Connemara by Alcock and Brown.

Denys was the only son of wealthy London barrister William and Ada (née Corbett) Wilson and was educated at Eton from 1896 to 1899. He served in the Boer War, having been commissioned into the Dorset Regiment, and in 1908 became a Lieutenant in the Royal Artillery. He was brash and egotistical and used his father's fortune to pursue his interests of horse racing, motor racing and flying. Denys also had a fascination with new technologies and had a pioneering spirit – common among rich young Edwardians.

Corbett-Wilson took flying lessons in the Blériot Flying School at Pau in southern France in 1911. When he received his aviator's certificate in 1912 he purchased a single-seater *Blériot XI*, a pioneering French-designed wood-and-fabric monoplane. Louis Blériot gained lasting fame in 1909 when he was the first to cross the English Channel in a similar heavier-than-air aircraft from Calais to Dover.

The challenge to cross the Irish Sea was first taken up two years earlier on 11 September 1910 by English actor-aviator Robert Loraine. He flew a *Farman* biplane, departing Holyhead at 11.05am and intending to land in the Phoenix Park. But his engine cut out five times on the journey and 90 minutes later, within sight of the Baily Lighthouse in Howth, it stalled for the last time. He ditched into the sea only 200 yards from the coast and had to swim ashore.

Denys Corbett-Wilson made his attempt on 17 April 1912. He challenged his Limerick-born friend Damer Allen to a race across the Irish Sea. Corbett-Wilson had met Allen, who had also only recently qualified to fly, at Hendon Aerodrome in north London. They both flew a *Blériot XI*, which had a compass but few other navigational aids. It had a maximum speed of about 65 miles per hour but was vulnerable in windy conditions.

Both took off from Hendon early in the morning in strong winds, which showed no sign of abating. Allen made it to Chester but Corbett-Wilson was forced to land at Hereford, having lost his compass in the wind. He checked into the Mitre Hotel for the night. Next day, rather than wait for his mechanic who was following by train, he topped up the engine with castor oil, which was used at the time, that he bought in a local chemist shop. He took off, only to land again a short distance away with engine trouble because the oil was the wrong grade.

Meanwhile, Allen had continued on to Holyhead and the next day attempted his flight to Ireland. But tragically his plane disappeared over the Irish Sea. He was never seen again and his body was never recovered. Newspaper reports at the time claimed that Corbett-Wilson and Allen had a wager on their race to Ireland but that was later denied.

Denys Corbett-Wilson, the first man to successfully fly from Britain to Ireland.

Corbett-Wilson crash-landed his Blériot XI in a field north-east of Enniscorthy.

Corbett-Wilson abandoned his plan to fly from Holyhead because of bad weather and decided instead to attempt the flight from Fishguard to County Wexford. Six days after Allen's failed attempt, he took off from a field at Goodwick, Fishguard at 5.47am on the morning of Monday 22 April 1912. One hour and forty minutes later, having flown into deteriorating weather conditions and with an erratic compass and misfiring engine, he landed in a field in the townland of Crane, north-east of Enniscorthy, in heavy rain. He thought the field that he chose to come down in was suitable but it proved too small and he ran into thick hedging, breaking the propeller. This was the first crossing of the Irish Sea from Britain to Ireland by aeroplane.

Denys became a local celebrity in the district and later that day he sent a telegram home saying: 'I have flown successfully St. George's Channel, starting from Fishguard at six o'clock and landing near Enniscorthy, Wexford County, in pouring rain and fog.' The damaged aeroplane was put into storage in stables on Lord Donoughmore's Estate. When the estate was sold years later, the plane was bought and later apparently donated to a museum in Kilkenny.

That week in April 1912 proved to be a busy time for pilots trying to make it across the Irish Sea. Just four days after Denys Corbett-Wilson's successful flight, it was the turn of millionaire Welsh pilot Captain Vivian Hewitt. He had planned to make the attempt the day before Corbett-Wilson but had to postpone it because of dense fog. He finally took off from a field near Rhyl in North Wales on 26 April and flew 75 miles in foggy conditions, landing 90 minutes later in the Phoenix Park. He later wrote in his logbook: 'Passage very rough and the wind strong and the machine took some handling.'

The newspapers in April 1912, however, were consumed by the enormous tragedy of the sinking of the *Titanic*. This meant that the heroic achievements of Denys Corbett-Wilson and Vivien Hewitt did not receive the recognition they deserved.

At the outbreak of WWI two years later, Corbett-Wilson immediately volunteered for the newly-created Royal Flying Corps. He served with No. 3 Squadron and on 10 May 1915 he and his observer were on a reconnaissance mission over France. Flying a *Morane-Saulnier L*, a two-seater scout plane, they were hit by German artillery and both killed. Denys, aged 32, was buried by the German army with full military honours near Lille. After the war, his remains were moved to the British War Cemetery at Cabaret-Rouge near Arras.

In April 2012, to mark the centenary of Denys Corbett-Wilson's achievement, memorial plaques were unveiled at the landing site in Crane and at Enniscorthy Castle, where an exhibition, 'The Life and Times of Corbett-Wilson' was held. There was also a fly-past by the Irish Air Corps and vintage aircraft from Enniscorthy and the UK. A play specially written by Derek Webb, '100 Minutes', was performed in both Fishguard's Theatr Gwaun and Wexford Arts Centre.

A Blériot XI, made of wood and canvas, similar to the plane flown by Corbett-Wilson in 1912. The photograph shows the Swiss aviator Oskar Bider, the first man to fly over the Alps in both directions, taking off from Bern in 1913 for his flight to Milan.

Capturing street life at the beginning of the 1900s

Delivery boys beside the Pikeman statue in the Bullring, an example of documentary photography in Wexford. The boy in the centre was delivering for Cooper's Medical Hall of 43 North Main Street while advertising their name around town.

IN THE LATE 19th century the railway from Dublin was extended to Wexford, but Wexford Harbour was in decline, with shipping transferring to the new

Robert French was chief photographer for the William Lawrence Studio in Dublin from 1880 until 1914.

port of Rosslare. In 1898, the whole town was decorated for the 1798 Rebellion centenary celebrations and the Pikeman statue was finally unveiled in the Bullring in 1905. The Boer War was raging in South Africa between 1899 and 1902 with the Wexford Militia taking part. John Redmond from Kilrane was elected leader of the Irish Parliamentary Party in 1900 and was campaigning for Home Rule.

But for most, everyday life continued in the town and this was captured in some fine documentary photographs taken by Robert French, who worked with the William Lawrence photographic studio of Sackville Street in Dublin. Lawrence opened his studio in his mother's fancy goods shop opposite the GPO in 1865 and employed French in 1880 as his chief photographer. Robert French travelled the length and breadth of Ireland, capturing landscapes and documenting life in almost every town and village, taking over 30,000 photographs. Many of them became printed postcards after 1902, when the Post Office introduced the 'divided back' postcard, which allowed people to write messages on one half of the back of the card and an address on the other half, with a picture on the front.

During the 1916 Easter Rising, the studio was looted and burnt down and glass plate negatives destroyed. However, the scenes taken around Ireland by Robert French had been stored for safe-keeping in Rathmines and survived the rebellion. In 1943, the National Library acquired the negatives and the following restored photograph details are taken from the collection.

(all photographs © National Library of Ireland)

Bringing home the messages on a summer's day in The Faythe. The thatched house on the far left is long gone and is now the site of the Gun Shop.

Fashionable ladies on North Main Street.

A sunny day on South Main Street. Sinnott's later became Woolworth's. Today, Sinnott's and Connick Provision Stores together make up Penney's department store.

Manning the Toll House at Ferrycarrig Bridge.

The Royal Irish Constabulary operated out of two police barracks in the town, one near the corner of Abbey Street and George's Street and the other on South Main Street (now Dún Mhuire Theatre).

*A smartly turned out constable outside Byrne's public house (later Cullen's clothes shop)
at 16 North Main Street.*

Hanging out in the Bullring.

Byrne's, formerly the Church of Ireland rectory and believed to be the birthplace of Lady Wilde, was later Lambert's Bar and is now Diana Donnelly boutique.

Posing with the postman outside Castlebrige Post Office.

At Ferrybank, near the site of the old wooden Wexford Bridge which was replaced in 1866 by Carcur Bridge.

Outside St. Iberius Church, young boys in knee-length breeches.

Men and women of all classes wore hats. Working men wore cloth caps, middle class men wore bowler hats and wealthy men wore top hats. All men wore three-piece suits.

Bibliography

Books

Carey, Tim, *Hanged for Murder* (Cork, 2013)

Colfer, Billy, *Wexford - a Town and its Landscape* (Cork, 2008)

Doyle, Ian (Ed.) and Browne, Bernard (Ed.), *Medieval Wexford* (Dublin, 2016)

Dwyer, T. Ryle, *Guests of the State* (Dingle, 1994)

Forde, Frank, *The Long Watch* (Dublin, 1981)

Forde, Rev. Walter (Ed.), *The Castlebridge Story* (Wexford, 2009)

Griffiths, George, *Chronicles of the County Wexford* (Enniscorthy, 1877)

Joyce, Patrick, *A Concise History of Ireland* (1910)

Lewis, Samuel, *A Topographical Dictionary of Ireland* (London, 1837)

Rossiter, Nicky, *My Wexford* (Dublin, 2006)

Rossiter, Nicky, *The Streets of Wexford* (Dublin, 2009)

Rowe, David and Scallan, Eithne, *Houses of Wexford* (Clare, 2004)

Whelan, Kevin (Ed.), *Wexford: History and Society* (Dublin, 1987)

Newspapers

Enniscorthy Guardian

Gorey Guardian

Irish Press

Irish Times

New Ross Standard

Wexford Free Press

Wexford Herald

Wexford Independent

Wexford People

Other sources

Bureau of Military History

Flight Safety Foundation

flightglobal.com

History Ireland

Inland Waterways Association of Ireland

Irish Arts Review

Irish Military Archives

National Folklore Collection/Dúchas

National Inventory of Architectural Heritage

National Library of Ireland

National Museum of Ireland

Rosslare Historical Society

theirishstory.com

The Scots Magazine

University of Cambridge

Wexford County Library

Made in the USA
Monee, IL
04 November 2022

17119819R00125